Blessed
Be the Bond

Blessed be the Bond

Christian Perspectives on Marriage and Family

William Johnson Everett

UNIVERSITY
PRESS OF
AMERICA

Lanham • New York • London

Copyright © 1990 by
University Press of America®, Inc.
4720 Boston Way
Lanham, Maryland 20706

3 Henrietta Street
London WC2E 8LU England

Copyright © 1985 originally by Fortress Press

Library of Congress Cataloging-in-Publication Data

Everett, William Johnson.
Blessed be the bond : Christian perspectives on marriage and family /
William Johnson Everett.
p.   cm.
Reprint, with new pref. Originally published: Philadelphia :
Fortress Press, 1985.
1. Marriage—Religious aspects—Christianity.
2. Family—Religious life.   I. Title.
BV835.E93   1989   234'.165—dc20   89–27347 CIP

ISBN 0–8191–7640–0

Blessed be the bond!
God praise the manna mortar
  binding stones along foundations
  of our tabernacled love!
Baptize the dusty desert
  of our wanderlusting hearts!
Pour gushing osculated wine
  upon the friendship of our lips!
God bless the bond of peace!

Contents

Preface to the University Press of America Edition   xi
Preface   xiii

1. The Social Experience   1

     Introduction: The Faith Challenge   1

     The Four Subjects of Marriage   2

         Person   3

         Couple   3

         Family   4

         Household   5

     The Subjects: From Fusion to Distinction   6

     The Challenge to Religion   10

2. The Framework of Theological Engagement   15

     The Symbolic Interchange   16

     Theological Roots of the Engagement   18

     Purposes and Motives of Marriage   20

         Purposes   20

         Motives   21

3. Symbols of Engagement   25

     The Symbolic Model   25

The Christian Symbols   26
The Models   29

4. Symbolic Models in Transition   35

    Marriage as Sacrament   37
    Marriage as Vocation   41
    Marriage as Covenant   44
    Marriage as Communion   50

5. Winnowing the Harvest   57

    The Social Experience   57
        The Transitions   57
        The Bonds of Marriage and Family   58
    The Guiding Values   60
        Personal Motives   60
            Expression and Confirmation   61
            Motives and Models   62
            Love, Sex, and Sacrifice   68
        Societal Purposes   71
        Ecclesial Purposes   75

    The Key Symbols in Theological Perspective   80
        Theological Foundations: Nature and Grace   81
        Faith: The Trustworthy Relationship   86

6. A Contemporary Theology of Marriage   91

    Marriage Is Natural   92
        A Natural Metaphor for Faith   92
        Marital Nature: From Substance to Action   93
        Marriage as Communicative Union   93

    Marriage as Communion   94
        The Grace of Empowering Resonance   94
        Conjugal Friendship: The Model of Equality   96

Personal Identity in Communion   97
From Communion to Covenant   100

Covenanted Communion   100
   The Marital Covenant   102
   The Parental Covenant   104

Marital Vocation: The Societal Covenant   111

Church as Sacrament of Marital Vocation   116

Contemporary Marriage and Family: Prospect and
   Practice   121
   Personal Nurture   122
   Weddings   124
   Profession: Public Vocation   125
   Profession: Parental Vocation   126

Preface
to
The University Press of America
Edition

Since this little volume appeared in 1985 it has found wide use in courses concerned with the ethical and religious dimensions of marriage and family life. A companion volume, in which I fill out its public and theological dimensions, has subsequently appeared as *God's Federal Republic: Reconstructing Our Governing Symbol* (Paulist Press, 1988).

Because people are putting together coupling, parenting and care for their elders in different ways we need to think more precisely and imaginatively about the patterns we practice and the purposes we pursue. This book presents a way we can think about these profound loyalties as well as a proposal for ordering them in our own time. To do this it provides both a language for naming the intricate obligations and meanings of domestic dynamics and a framework for sorting out and comparing the enduring ways people approach them.

This approach has proven useful for people studying ethics, theology, family life and the psychology or sociology of religion. It has also helped pastoral counselors and professionals in ministry or family care respond to the issues and difficulties people experience in this often turbulent realm. It provides ways of bringing their own responses into line with the way people think, feel, talk and pray about their marriages and families.

Teachers will want to supplement it with further clinical, scientific, ethical or theological materials, not to mention the insights and wisdom arising from their own practical experience. Students will need to take time for discussion and argument in order to apply its categories to their own perspectives and experiences.

As a basis for general reading it can help older people put together their life experience in a more integrated way by supplying names and connections for their vital experiences. For younger people, it can serve as a checklist for identifying points of resonance and dissonance in their emerging relationships with lovers and mates. All of us can use it to chart our relationships with our parents and look at the way we are parents to the next generation.

In very brief compass this book offers a language for talking about the intricate relationships that give our lives their vital bonds as well as their constricting bondage. It is up to each reader to use it to construct the narrative for her or his own life.

William Johnson Everett
Atlanta
1989

Preface

For the past ten years I have been wading, indeed floundering, in the vast gulf between our inherited theologies of marriage and the actual experiences probed by the behavioral sciences. This book is an effort to present a theological position fully informed by a critical appropriation of the social sciences. The churches' attention to these issues has either dwelt in the lofty ideals derived from faith positions or enthusiastically grabbed onto whatever recent therapeutic device might seem to help people struggle through their difficulties or maximize their marital and familial happiness. What has been missing is a coherent theory that would rigorously critique our sloppy invocation of high ideals as well as our eclectic advocacy of the latest psychological tool. This book is an effort to order our theological reflection in a systematic way that can give us some leverage for dealing with these complex and emotional issues.

I am convinced that an adequate approach to these matters drives us back to some fundamental reformulations of our understanding of people as well as of faith. I am presently writing a longer volume that lays out this basic framework. This short book presupposes many of those ideas, but without much elaboration. I have simply used them with the least possible amount of explanation in order to accomplish the more limited goals of this presentation.

As a theoretical effort, it does not survey the existing practices for dealing with family problems. This information we have in copious quantities, much of it excellent. While I do not dwell on these practical matters, however, I do offer numerous entrees to them. These suggestions for following up issues are contained in the Notes at the ends of chapters.

Many influences coalesce in this essay. I have been enriched and challenged by students and colleagues at St. Francis Seminary, especially Arthur Heinze, Andrew Nelson, Kenneth Smits, Kenneth Metz, and Martin Pable, as well as an earlier collaborator, T. J. Bachmeyer. My own experience in marriage, parenthood, and divorce has forged the emotional structure of my thought. With my children I have known the resilience of parental bonds. Most important, through the bond of love with my precious wife Sylvia I have come to know the riches of marital communion.

Milwaukee   William Johnson Everett
June 1984

1

The Social Experience

bonds

breaking apart

INTRODUCTION: THE FAITH CHALLENGE

Our lives arise in the bonds created by our forebears. We come to fullness of life through the bonds we ourselves create with others as well as with the world around us. When they are shattered so are we. When they are strong and resilient so are we. Nothing is more fundamental to our life than the affirmation of the bonds that bless our lives. Of all these bonds the bond of marriage has been held most dear and has received most fully the blessing of the church.

The problem we sense acutely is that these bonds, especially those of marriage, have changed radically in recent generations. Moreover, we find our bonds tearing us apart as their objects fly in opposite directions. Or the bonds of our ancestors are a bondage to us. We find ourselves torn between bonds and blessings, between the affirmations of faith and the life we really lead. Many of these dilemmas come to rest within the problem of living out a faithful life in our marriages and families. This essay is a response to the challenge of finding blessings in the building of our bonds.

Uncle Remus has given us the timeless story of Br'er Rabbit's attack on the mocking tar baby set up by Br'er Fox. Once he had hit this puppet of tar, he was trapped. The more he struck the insolent dummy the more embroiled and stuck he became, much to the delight of Br'er Fox.

Marriage and family are the church's tar baby. Intense ambivalence has always characterized their relationship. Indeed, the ministry of Jesus was largely indifferent to it as he tried to focus on

a transcendent renewal of creation. Once Christians started to
come to terms with married life, either to accept it or to change it,
however, Christianity became embroiled in a controversy it has
never resolved. Indeed, this is probably a dilemma impossible of
resolution.

The controverted character of this embroilment arises from
many sources—the paradoxes and dilemmas of married life itself,
the tension between "the way the world is" and the intimations of
a faith vision, and the sheer variety of ways that churches and
societies seek a vital engagement with each other. The challenge to
a faithful engagement with marital life is many-sided. It demands
an examination of social and psychological experience as well as of
faith and theology.

Marriage is no longer a solo ballet in which one dancer plays all
the parts. It is a dance of many partners—each distinctive, each
with its unique role. This essay is an effort to engage this ensemble
as a rich complexity, while at the same time preserving the original
meanings of the dance.

Our first step is sociological. We must understand the patterns
of our actual existence. Therefore, we shall first distinguish four
"subjects" of discourse—persons, couples, families, and households. These four subjects often intermix but play distinct roles in
the history of thinking about these matters and in forming religious responses to them. As our second step we must see the way
they have become differentiated from each other. Christianity has
contributed to this differentiation, often in unintended ways. The
increasing distinction among them, however, especially between
marriage and family, now requires Christians to reconstruct their
approach to marriage.

THE FOUR SUBJECTS OF MARRIAGE

The confusion of the four subjects is often manifested when we
seek to include singles in our family-life programs but do not know
whether we include them as family fragments, as households, or as
unactualized partners. Yet we feel somehow that we ought not
discuss family without them. At other times we are not sure what
the major issue is in divorce—the breakup of a family, a house-

hold, a couple, or a person. To clarify our language and meaning, we have to describe each of these subjects.

Person

By "person" we mean an individual with rights, duties, powers, and status apart from any relation with spouse, parents, children, relatives, or household. We do not mean a mere individual as such, since the individual as a body has always existed. We mean a social construct that sees this individual as a public and social reality in his or her own right. Because we have come to see these rights as inalienable we forget that they are cultural assumptions arising from conviction rather than biology.[1]

This conception of person has been nourished by biblical and classical traditions. It is a social outcome of the concept of the soul created in the image of God. It has intertwined with the Roman concept of "persona," by which the self gained a publicly acknowledged reality in law and politics. The concept of persona became identified with godhead by Tertullian, Augustine, and later Western Trinitarians. It subsequently brought its divine dignity back down to earth, bestowing the virtues of creativity, ultimacy, authority, and power on individuals. The rise of philosophies of personality in the eighteenth and nineteenth centuries gave us the cultural base for speaking of persons and personalities that have their value directly from God, rather than from their sexual, familial, or domestic status.

Today we take this idea of the self as a person for granted, but it is a social construct that has taken two millennia to reach its present state. In our own time we are reifying it in laws and economic contracts, as well as in our image of marriage and family. Its impact on theology and ministry has been immense, so much so that almost everyone focuses on the primacy of the person, even though they disagree violently on the proper social relationships by which personality is achieved and preserved.

Couple

A "couple," from this perspective, is the union of two persons. Of course in patriarchal times the equality connoted by this term was absent. In that case the wife emerged as the body of the male

—his body to do with as he wished, whether for good or ill. The woman was merely a receptacle for his seed, sparing him the confinement and misery of childbirth so that he could engage in warfare and public affairs. Nevertheless, in all times there has been some acknowledgment that there was a couple as such, even though this may have been restricted to the nobility, or, without much mention, to those too poor to maintain the conventions of patriarchy.

In the concept of marriage as a personal contract we see the effort, in the first millennium, to differentiate the couple from the family, making the marriage a matter of free consent rather than family prerogative. This struggle for marriage as free contract was always intense as long as the fourfold fusion of person, couple, family, and household held sway. As a contract, marriage became a matter of public law rather than blood feud. As a personal contract, it became, at least in theory, a voluntary relation between two equals, even though they may have been unequal in every other way. With such faint beginnings we see the birth of personal dignity and the independence of the couple from the family and clan.

In our own time this couple is an emotional unity characterized by bonding and communion as well as by being a legal entity firmly entrenched in statute and revenue codes. To be a couple still has status advantages, as most single persons can attest. Generally, it is this subject that we think of when we speak of marriage. It is only very recently, however, that the couple as such had a possible and expected durability apart from family. This has only been possible because of contraception and health care—factors I shall discuss later.

Family

Sometimes people speak of a couple as a family, but most of the time "family" means children—daughters and sons, brothers and sisters, mothers and fathers. By extension it means grandmothers and grandfathers, aunts and uncles, cousins, nieces, and nephews. This is family—the network of relationships established by birth, marriage, and the artificial birth of adoption.

The pattern of these relationships and the rights and duties attaching to these various roles differs greatly according to culture, class, religion, and region.[2] This is why all talk of "the family" is really the projection of an ideal rather than an empirical description. Just as the relationships between spouses vary greatly today, so do those in families.

Some notion of family, however, no matter what its content, remains very important to most people and especially to the institutions of government, economics, and religion, which relate to people as members of families.

Household

A "household" is a domestic organization occupying a specific space—be it an apartment, a single dwelling unit, or a palace. In the past the household may have also included servants, slaves, and apprentices as well as various relatives.[3] The household is an economic organization. Today it is mostly a consumptive one—taking in processed goods to be used or displayed by the members of the household. In former times, and in all agricultural cultures, it has been a productive enterprise—engaged in producing food.

A family is not necessarily the same as a household. The members of a family need not occupy the same household, just as the members of a household may not all be members of the same family. Children have often lived away from their parents after the age of ten. In our own time divorce has created two-household families in which children participate in varying degrees in the households of both their separated parents. We still speak of single-parent families when we mean single-parent households, however. Our language, like our thought, has not kept up with reality.

In feudal times, households were traditionally parts of an estate, a *patrimonium*. The function of the family was to care for the *patrimonium*, which may have included productive property as well as financial assets, rights, and titles. Many of these attached to the land and the house as such. The family held these properties only through the household and its estate. In our own time, of course, this attachment to the land has been broken almost completely. Property rights inhere in the persons, who may hold them individually or jointly, depending on their preference or the laws of the state they reside in.

THE SUBJECTS:
FROM FUSION TO DISTINCTION

It should already be evident that these four subjects have often been conflated with one another, or to put the matter more nostalgically, their original unity has broken down. The image we probably have of the medieval European family is such an identification.

In this image, the couple, lacking contraception, immediately generated children and became a family. Of course this procreation also arose from a desire to combat the high mortality rate, ensure an adequate supply of cheap labor, and provide for offspring to care for them if by extreme good fortune they arrived at the blessing of senility. Sometimes the children came first. People could get married—form a couple—only after they could form a household. This was especially true where all available land had been assigned.

At that time (and this is still the case in many regions of the world), to speak of one of the subjects was to speak of them all. Thus, our traditional term for marriage, "Holy Matrimony," actually means "motherhood," or "that which is created by the mother." That is, marriage was simply "family making." When a prelate blessed a marriage he was also blessing a family (*matrimonium*) and a household (*patrimonium*). He was legitimating the formation of an enterprise central to the economic, social, and governmental welfare of the people as a whole. To this day the nuptial blessing bears its marks as a prayer for the bride's faithfulness and fertility.

Ivan Illich has recently drawn our attention to the way "the house" of the medieval manor, like that of biblical times, was a transcendent reality into which generations of couples entered in order to maintain the land. In that context marriage was simply the legal format for maintaining the house. This manifests the meaning of household as the subject of marriage.

When households were the real subject of marriage, property relations were the real concern of the church. Through marriage the church was seeking to achieve social order and justice by stabilizing the feudal mosaic of households. It was through the household, and therefore through their marriage, that individuals really could become "persons," that is, actors in the public realm.

With this fusion of the subjects, it is little wonder that today we have such trouble sorting out what the church's concern really was when it got involved with marriage.

In the last few centuries the four subjects of marriage have differentiated from each other.[4] What was once a stellar fusion has exploded into a complex constellation. This is the fundamental sociological fact guiding the reconstruction of a Christian approach to marriage in our time.

This differentiation of subjects, an uneven and halting development in many ways, rested on medical and economic changes as well as on the force of cultural and religious convictions. Religion, of course, did as much to preserve the fusion of the four subjects as to break them apart. These three social forces—medicine, economics, and religion—played out their power in various ways in the midst of enormous migrations, the displacement of war, and decimation by disease.

The shift from an agricultural to an industrial economy broke the relation between household and productive economic life. The household became a unit of consumption. Its economic function was to supply workers for enterprises outside the home. These people worked primarily as individuals, not as families. Therefore, the split between household and economy advanced the distinction between person and family, although in most cases this was a negative development in which men, women, and children were exploited through individual labor contracts. On the positive side, the rise of "rational organizations," which rewarded people on the basis of individual performance, made it possible for some people to redress the power imbalance they may have experienced in the traditional family and household.

The rise of national and global corporations, along with their far-flung labor markets, created a mobility that further distinguished individuals from a family household. Millions of migrant workers wander the earth today—some poor and some very wealthy. Of course, modern forms of communication make it possible to maintain a high degree of family awareness, even though this does not operate through households. In this case, however, the family functions to give a sense of identity and support, not to produce goods for the marketplace.

The transition from agriculture to industry has also been a move from labor-intensive to capital-intensive production. This means that procreation is not as important. Rather than being an asset, children become the consumers of family resources devoted primarily to securing schooling for them so that they can take part in an increasingly technological civilization. This schooling is a particularly nonfamilial form of education. The family, which in all agricultural times and among artisans as well has been the locus for education, now loses this function to an independent organization associated with the government or nonprofit corporations.

This loss of function and the concomitant specialization in independent institutions of education, health care, life insurance, nursing homes, social security, and the like, characterizes the last four centuries of family life in the West. The differentiation of education has given children a place of independence from their parents. The rise of social security and institutions for the elderly has preserved this distance in later life. The development of a rational economy has given both women and men opportunities for independence, expanding the personal powers of many, though, we must add, at the cost of much economic suffering and inequality.

This differentiation was first of all economic and political. Families may have become more distant in terms of household relations but have become emotionally closer in personal ways. Intimacy has risen while relations of power and authority have diminished. Families, as almost everyone attests, have become arenas of intimacy and friendship, even between generations. In Christopher Lasch's words, they have become "havens in a heartless world."[5]

The second major factor differentiating the four subjects, especially in the last fifty years, has been medical. We must remember that the human ovum was not even identified until 1827, and the cycle of ovulation was not understood until the end of that century.[6] Nevertheless, birthrates fell steadily throughout the century. Long before contraceptives gained widespread use, the decline of infant mortality made high birthrates unnecessary. Voluntary restraint was widely practiced in industrial areas as well as in agricultural places like Ireland, where lack of householding possibilities had always kept the age of marriage high and the birthrate low. Similar economic constraints exercised their impact on birthrates in other areas as well. The fall in birthrates accompanied and made possible the increasing independence of women, their demand for companionship as equals, and a greater attention to the unique needs of children for nurture.

Medical advances also increased longevity, so that people could begin to look forward to a time when they would live as a couple apart from their children, who had left to follow careers and independent lives. This development increased the expectation that marriage should serve the interests of long-term friendship rather than procreation or production.

Contraception not only freed the couple from becoming a family, but also freed women from being simply the productive appendage of the man. They could then develop their own personhood outside the household. Contraception thus had a threefold effect of differentiating person from couple, person from household, and couple from family. Little wonder that it has been so opposed by those who had sanctified their earlier fusion.

Carl Degler argues that the nineteenth century was the turning point in the development of the modern family. At the same time that the personhood of women was being established separate from men, the family, and the household, other medical and economic changes were providing women with the power that made possible a genuinely equal relation with men. On the basis of equality men and women could become intimate friends rather than functionaries of a procreative or productive household.

This is not to say that the movement from a patriarchal to an egalitarian marriage has been a simple one. We must note that the meaning of patriarchy in the agricultural family, where the woman was a part of productive enterprise, was quite different from patriarchy in the industrial bourgeois family, where she was a symbol of the father/husband's power and affluence. In the farm family spouses and children had a systemic, organic relationship in which they exercised interdependent functional roles. This is the model of patriarchy taken up by the church, using the Pauline body model. The rule of the husband in the family isolated from productive enterprise was more clearly dualistic, however. The woman had no economic power unless she could rely on dowry money. Here we find the naked hierarchy in which the woman's function is strictly to symbolize male power—even to the point of hiding the sexual function by which she produced babies. This is the specific form of sexism attacked by the feminist movements that arose at the turn of the century.

In short, the original fusion of the four subjects has given way to their differentiation under the impact of economic, cultural, and scientific changes. The creation of our relationships as persons, couples, families, and households is more and more a voluntary matter. Individuals do not have to get married to have a social position. Couples do not have to have children, for whatever reason. Moreover, families do not necessarily constitute a single household. To be sure, there are powerful cultural forces that press people to create a familial household and intimate relationships, but it is not the matter of necessity it once was.

THE CHALLENGE TO RELIGION

The various world religions differ in their relationship to marriage and family life.[7] Some have arisen as the symbolic expression of family ideals themselves—they are a part of family life. There is essentially no difference between family and religion, or at least between religion and the extended family of the ethnic group. Others, like Buddhism, see marital life as indifferent or hostile to the achievement of religious ideals.

Christianity's relationship is fundamentally ambivalent. On the one hand, it is ethically committed to honoring marital relationships, a position anchored in Jesus' prohibition of divorce.[8] It is, however, also profoundly suspicious of family ties as impediments to true holiness. Monastic asceticism epitomizes this pole of Christian life. The first expression of profound ambivalence is St. Paul's admonition to Christians awaiting the imminent end of the age: "From now on, let those who have wives live as though they had none . . . " (1 Cor. 7:29); "he who marries his betrothed does well; and he who refrains from marriage will do better" (1 Cor. 7:38). For Paul, then, the question of marriage and family obligations was neutralized in light of the ultimate question of "how to please the Lord."

In the course of the next millennium, however, Christianity took on a general care of the whole society. The ethic of ascetic indifference and even hostility was institutionalized in the monastery while the ethic of family obligation and honor was developed into a natural law of family life.[9] By the twelfth century we find not only a lofty affirmation of ascetic flight from the world but also a towering edifice of matrimonial sacramentality. The poles of ambivalence had been isolated into twin pillars of the church.

The condensation of Christianity's understanding of marriage as a sacrament occurred in this late medieval period. It therefore reflects and indeed is built upon the patterns of marital and family life existing at that time. Fundamentally, these were patterns in which the four subjects were tightly conjoined. Moreover, because the whole society revolved around kinship bonds, the church could exercise its general social concern through this one complex institution of marriage. By controlling the terms by which people become a couple, it could seek to control families, households, the economy, and the feudal arrangements sustaining them. Control of the marriage contract was a matter of general social justice, seen from the standpoint of that time. This reasoning depended on the fusion of the four subjects. It is a reasoning we find almost unfathomable in our own setting, where these have become distinct from each other.

Societal changes require a complete rethinking of our approach to marriage as a sacrament. This is a more complicated endeavor than some might think. It involves not only a redefinition of marriage but also of the general relationship of church to society as well as the theological foundations for this relationship. This essay is a contribution to that complex reconstruction. It attempts to provide a framework for rethinking these relationships.

This task requires more than simply a reconsideration of marriage as a sacrament. Christianity is also heir to other approaches to marriage, especially those arising out of the Reformation. Here the claim of sacramentality was denied, but marriage was still conceived as an ethically and religiously significant institution. It was not simply an alternative opposed to the ascetic ideal of celibacy. Marriage was to become an arena for saintliness, whether to manifest faithful love (Lutherans) or to act as an instrument for transforming the world (Calvinists). Marriage itself was still sanctified, even if not sanctifying.

While this development, so visible in the cultural impact of Puritanism in the American colonies, contributed to the modern differentiation of the four subjects, it was also bound to its social origins. The contemporary situation is not merely a child and heir of the Puritan ideal. It is a stranger and a challenger that requires us to rethink our approach to marriage as an exercise in faith or as an instrument of the Kingdom.

Sociological changes demand religious responses. At this point we can see that the constellation of the four subjects has moved from being a functional system to a more pluralistic collection of domestic possibilities. Patriarchal hierarchy has given way to intimate equality as an ideal. Personal fulfillment has taken increasing precedence over organizational solidarity as the under-lying social meaning of marriage and family life. Faith can no longer be seen simply as a way to find energy to fulfill traditional social roles. It must become a critical lever for entering into the new possibilities we face today.

Religious convictions also demand social changes, however. Enduring values must be retrieved and revitalized, though in new societal forms. Even these brief remarks indicate that the relation of religion and society has always been reciprocal. In affecting societal notions of contract, person, or vocation, the church has been conditioned in turn. The meaning of Christianity's key sym-bols can only be worked out with the cultural tools people have at hand. This is a dynamic process of reciprocal transformation.[10]

In the following chapters we will explore the intricate ways that changes in the four subjects are intertwined with changes in the church's primary symbols of marriage—as contract, covenant, sac-rament, or communion. In pursuing this investigation it is impor-tant that we suspend as much as possible our preconceptions about these matters. Only by stepping back for a fresh look can we engage these radical changes free of clichéd exhortations or desic-cated commonplaces.

NOTES

1. The history of the word "person" goes back to the Latin word for mask, and perhaps an earlier Etruscan term for a harlequin figure who led the dead through ritual trial into the other world. Originally it involved the social means for entering into the nonnatural world of the drama, then by extension into legal relationships beyond the family. In

Christian theology it came to depict the presence of God in creation, Christ, and the church. By extension it then began to designate church figures (hence our word "parson"), public figures, and through subsequent democratization all citizens, that is, all human beings. See Gordon Allport's overview of this history in *Personality: A Psychological Interpretation* (New York: Henry Holt, 1937), chap. 2. Also Edward Schillebeeckx and Bas van Iersel, eds., *A Personal God?* Concilium vol. 103 (New York: Seabury Press, 1977).

2. The definition of "family" is besieged by problems, as any standard text reveals. See Arlene Skolnick, *The Intimate Environment: Exploring Marriage and the Family* (2d ed.; Boston: Little, Brown & Co., 1973), chap. 2. In *Critical Theory of the Family* (New York; Seabury Press, 1978), Mark Poster distinguishes between bourgeois, aristocratic, peasant, and working-class families.

3. A classic source for ancient Roman family life is still Numa Denis Fustel de Coulanges, *The Ancient City* (Garden City, N.Y.: Doubleday Anchor Books, [1864]), book II. Ivan Illich offers some helpful historical insights in *Gender* (New York: Pantheon Books, 1982).

4. Differentiation is central to Talcott Parsons's work. I am treating family as he treated religion in "Christianity and Modern Industrial Society," in *Sociological Theory and Modern Society* (New York: Free Press, 1967), 385–421. For his influential views on family, see *Social Structure and Personality* (New York: Free Press, 1964), chaps. 1–3; and Hyman Rodman, "Parsons' View of the Changing American Family," in *Perspectives in Marriage and the Family,* ed. J. R. Eshleman (Boston: Allyn & Bacon, 1969), 93–112.

Parsons's student, Robert Bellah, worked out the implications for comparative religion in "Religious Evolution," *American Sociological Review* 29 (1964): 358–74. For a discussion of the industrial and technological revolutions, see William Goode, "World Revolution and Family Patterns," in *The Family in Transition: Rethinking Marriage, Sexuality, Child Rearing and Family Organization,* ed. Arlene Skolnick and Jerome Skolnick (Boston: Little, Brown, & Co., 1977), 111–21.

5. Christopher Lasch, *Haven in a Heartless World: The Family Besieged* (New York: Basic Books, 1977).

6. Carl Degler's *At Odds: Women and the Family in America from the Revolution to the Present* (New York and London: Oxford University Press, 1980) is a very helpful resource for the sociological dimensions of our project, though I stress the importance of public action itself, while he focuses on the individual autonomy necessary for it. For the medical history, see chap. 9. Theresa Sullivan points out the significance of longevity for intimacy in "Numbering Our Days Aright: Human Longevity and the Problem of Intimacy," in *The Family: In Crisis or in Transition? A Sociological and Theological Perspective,* Concilium vol. 121 (New York: Seabury Press, 1979).

7. More research needs to be done on family in comparative religious studies. For a historical-comparative approach, see Bernard I. Murstein, *Love, Sex, and Marriage Throughout the Ages* (New York: Springer Publishing, 1974). On the sociological side, see Gerald Leslie, *The Family in Social Context* (5th ed.; New York and London: Oxford University Press, 1982).

8. Among the many treatments of marriage and divorce in the Bible, see especially Myran and Robert Kysar, *The Asundered: Biblical Teachings on Divorce and Remarriage* (Atlanta: John Knox Press, 1978), and Donald W. Shaner, *A Christian View of Divorce According to the Teachings of the New Testament* (Leiden: E. J. Brill, 1969).

9. Recently, however, Jean LeClercq has gathered evidence of the simultaneous emergence of a more romantic view of marriage in *Monks on Marriage: A Twelfth-Century View* (New York: Seabury Press, 1982). Joseph Martos, *Doors to the Sacred: A Historical Introduction to Sacraments in the Catholic Church* (Garden City, N.Y.: Doubleday Image Books, 1982), chap. 11, offers an excellent history of the sacrament of marriage. Sebastian McDonald presents some fine-tooth reflections in "Theological Development of Marriage as a Sacrament," *Resonance* 4 (Spring 1967):87–117.

10. The methodology I am using behind the scenes to relate theology and the behavioral sciences is laid out in William W. Everett and T. J. Bachmeyer, *Disciplines in Transformation: A Guide to Theology and the Behavioral Sciences* (Washington, D.C.: University Press of America, 1979).

2

The Framework
of Theological Engagement

Christians, like everyone else, are faced with radical and decisive changes in the patterns of marriage, family life, and householding. We all face difficult choices in the complex dance of life these subjects perform around us. These choices need to be informed not only by our experience but by our faith. Yet in turning to our storeroom of props and costumes offered by the churches, we face diversity as well. Both in society and in Christianity we find various costumes, roles, and steps for this engagement.

We have already seen some of the crucial societal changes we must consider. Now we turn to the resources of faith. We find here a variety of basic approaches to faith, whether through cultic participation, prophetic proclamation, or ecstatic experience. Out of this history of Christian life and thought have arisen a number of key symbols that Christians employ for engaging marital reality—sacrament, covenant, communion, vocation, *ecclesiola* ("little church"), and Trinity, to cite only a few.

The engagement can assume many combinations. Sacrament can attach to the couple or the family. Covenant can focus on the household or couple. Vocation can be anchored in the person, the couple, or the family. Communion can occur among all family members or only between the spouses. The combinations are many. Each has had its own niche in the ecology of Christian life. We need to be sensitive to all of them. In this section, however, we will only explore combinations produced by four of the symbols

used by Christians over the centuries—sacrament, vocation, covenant, and communion.

In order to sort out this rich heritage and find out how to engage
our own social life in a faithful manner, we must first explore how
these basic symbols operate. What is the relationship between faith
symbols and marital life? Second, we must grasp the basic faith
concerns that underlie this engagement in the first place. Third, we
have to identify the main purposes and values Christians have tried
to pursue in working out a Christian engagement with marriage
and family. Finally, we need to clarify how these Christian symbols
are linked with social patterns to form symbolic models undergirding a particular faith approach to marriage. This chapter erects a
framework in response to these questions.

A complicated and difficult task lies ahead. We do not know
whether we will end up dancing in the briar patch or mired in a tar
baby. But it is an unavoidable endeavor for human beings who are
also trying to be people of faith. The only question is whether we
shall do it superficially or well.

THE SYMBOLIC INTERCHANGE

Each of these combinations forms a two-way street. Not only
does the church seek to make marriage a *symbol of* faith's mysteries, but married life itself yields up images which then become
metaphors for these mysteries of faith.[1] On the one hand, the
church has sought to make marriage and family mirror transcendent realities, such as God's love, Christ's relation to the church,
or God's covenant with Israel. It has sought to impose faith
realities on marriage. On the other hand, marital experience yields
up some of our most powerful symbols, which then help us express
the meaning of the ineffable transcendent.

This reciprocal exchange has occurred throughout biblical and
church history. The Song of Songs vividly employs marital experience in order to form our relationship of faith with God. The
story of Hosea uses the vicissitudes of a marriage to proclaim the
reality of Yahweh's faithfulness toward Israel. In the first case an
unabashed articulation of fervent love condenses into an image of
faith. In the second, a clear image of God finds expression through
one person's perseverance in marital fidelity.

We are not merely making an interesting intellectual distinction here. The direction of movement between marriage and faith reflects the practical and institutional dimensions of the relationship as well. When churches try to shape marriage, either through ecclesiastical discipline or civil legislation, they are usually trying to bring faith concepts to bear on marriage. Christian marriage is to be a symbol *of* faith. It is to manifest the faith of the church. Therefore, it must be indissoluble, or monogamous, or procreative, loving, intimate, and so forth, depending on the conception of faith at work.

When people try to reform church practices concerning weddings, divorce, sacramental participation, or parish programs, they are bringing actual marital experience in as a metaphor *for* faith. They are asking that faith be relevant to life, that it respect our natural experience of pilgrimage in brokenness and growth regardless of the religious conception of marriage we are using.

One of the most momentous scriptural passages exhibiting this reciprocity is the Pauline reflection on marriage and the mystery of faith in Eph. 5:21–33.[2] Here the sacrificial relationship of Christ to the church is first lifted up as a symbol to be expressed in marriage. The relationship of husband and wife is to be a symbol of Christ's relationship to the church. The woman is to be subjected to the man. The man is to sacrifice himself for the woman, protecting and guiding her. On this basis many Christians have defended a paternalistic model of marriage as a matter of faith, not merely of social custom.

Two other currents are also at work in this passage, however. First, it is clear that a certain conception of marital relationships has already informed the conception of church and of Christ. Just as the woman is the body of the man, so the church is the body of Christ. Just as women are unclean (reflecting taboos around menstruation and childbirth) so Christians are unclean until sanctified by Christ. Here we see, more implicitly, cultural conceptions of sexuality and marriage informing the proclamation of faith.

Second, Paul points to the hallowed observation that "a man shall leave his father and mother and be joined to his wife, and the two shall become one." He then says, "This mystery [Greek: *mysterion*] is a profound one, and I am saying that it refers to Christ and the church." At this point two things are going on. First, Paul is taking a marital reality of union and using it as a symbol for faith. The sense of both "metaphor for faith" and "symbol of faith" are operative with the choice of the word *mysterion,* however. On the one hand, it can mean simply that the marital union is awesome, or that the fact of leaving the parents, psychologically and physically, in order truly to marry someone is a great truth. In this case, it is a truth (a metaphor) *for* faith. As it worked out, however, *mysterion* was translated into the Latin as *sacramentum,* which already was coming to mean a definite symbol *of* faith. When that happened marriage was construed as a specific medium of grace, as much as preaching or baptizing. Over the centuries it was this notion of marriage as sacrament that shaped the Western church's approach.

All through our discussion, then, we will see this dialectic at work. Each direction has its own peculiar implications for our practices as well as our ultimate values. Each reflects the relative positions of influence among church, family, and other social institutions.

THEOLOGICAL ROOTS OF THE ENGAGEMENT

The traffic on this street is not only a product of shifts in the social or cultural character of Christianity or of married life. It also arises from tensions within theological discourse itself. This reciprocity reflects the dynamic interplay between nature and grace. This can also be expressed as the relation between creation and salvation, or between faith and reason. These are all angles of vision on a central theological problematic—namely, how to relate life as it is with how it can or ought to be.

Marriage and family are, first of all, *natural* institutions. That is, every society has some stable pattern for handling the long-term relationship of a man and a woman and for raising their offspring. It is simply part of the human condition. These patterns arise out of human needs and social convention. They are sustained to the degree that people are able to, given the objective circumstances of their life. When these given energies and resources fail us, the marriage or family fails. When they are present it blossoms freely.

From a religious standpoint, however, marriage is more than

grace
faith

this. It is a pattern rooted in the ultimate structure of things. It is to be sustained not merely by the energies we have but by our aspiration, conviction, and will. It is a *work of grace* as well as of nature. It is given to us to the extent that we have faith in God. It arises, first of all, from the power of grace, the life of the church, or Christ's relationship to the world. It is more the work of faith, hope, and charity than of our natural affection based in the peculiarities of our personalities. When we speak of this process as grace we emphasize the power coming from God. When we speak of it as faith we emphasize our own appropriation of it, either as the faith of the church or as our own personal spirituality.

Nature and grace point to two different vantage points for approaching marriage. Each Christian tradition finds its own way of relating the two.[3] Ascetics have pitted them against each other, so that marriage and family are heroic acts of shaping marital experience to fit faith convictions. Others find the nature of marriage leading us to and shaping faith reality. Eastern Orthodox theology seems to have a "two levels" approach, in which the religious reality exists as a heavenly permanence but the equally valid human and natural experience of marriage and divorce goes its own way without impugning the sacramental realities. This verges on an effort to hold them paradoxically together. Finally, we see the complex effort in Roman Catholic tradition to reshape nature to the demands of faith, first by seeing the natural institution through faith's eyes and then nurturing it toward its perfection, working at failures at the pastoral level but denying them at the institutional level.

The theological distinction between nature and grace resonates with psychological distinctions between *being* and *will.* On the one hand, we have our given psychological structure. Our emotions and deepest dispositions are developed long before we come to consciousness of them. Our relationships with parents, brothers, and sisters organize our ways of seeking and giving love. We see the world through the emotional filters developed in our earliest years. They constitute our psychological nature. This nature is our being.

Yet we also have a developed consciousness and sense of what we might become. We develop and shape our ideals about the world as well as our way of dealing with its inadequacies. We construct wider and wider concepts for a public beyond our intimate companions. We create a faith by which to move in a mysterious world.[4] Even in our personality, then, we evidence a melding of nature and grace, of the being we are and the will to change.

In all these efforts to bring together the dimensions of grace and nature Christians are tempted to dissolve these tensions by excluding one pole. They may so emphasize the demands of faith that they practically exclude marriage for genuine Christians. Or they so elevate natural marriage that people can no longer distinguish the faith experience in the center of their lives as married people. The difficult task is to piece together, in all of this complexity, some pathway that holds both landmarks in view.

The distinction between symbols *of* faith and metaphors *for* faith reflects this distinction between nature and grace. An emphasis on marriage as natural leads to seeing it as a generator of metaphors for faith. An emphasis on faith sees marriage as a symbol of faith. In the first, faith is an extrapolation from marital reality—its love, sacrifice, pain, or hope. In the second, faith manifests itself through marriage.

PURPOSES AND MOTIVES OF MARRIAGE

There is yet one more dimension to the interchange between the church and marriage—that formed by the arguments over the purposes of marriage. Lurking behind it is the issue of people's reasons and motives for entering marriage. Purposes refer more to matters of institutional and social policy. Motives refer to the psychology of individuals. Bringing the two together is no easy task.

Purposes

Discussion of the purposes of marriage arose as soon as Christians came to a general acceptance of it as a positive contribution to faith. The problem lay in discerning the social purposes that could be aligned with religious and ecclesiastical ones. Augustine saw three basic purposes in marriage—faith, children, and sacrament (*fides, proles, et sacramentum*).[5] Faith, of course, could mean many things, including simply the general observation (or mystery) that we deepen in faith through the joys and trials of married and family life. Faith soon came to be equated with permanence, however. A faith-full marriage was simply one in which the partners were married to each other until death.

Procreation was simply taken over from general cultural expectations. The early church was uninterested in procreation in light of the return of Christ. Appeals to the exhortation in Genesis to be fruitful and multiply, however, as well as later appeals to bring as many souls into heaven as possible provided enough cement to maintain this purpose as a Christian one.

Finally, and most obscurely, marriage was *sacramentum*. In part we have an appeal here to the Latin translation of Paul's *mysterion*, but we also have the introduction of the legal and contractual features of Roman law. *Sacramentum* contained the notion of sworn oath from its military use, and was a solemnly binding mutual obligation. Therefore, marriage had to have the content of a sworn oath between two people who were personally obligated to uphold it. Here we find the beginnings of an effort to bind marriage and church together at the point of worship if not ethical discipline. Marriage and family, by being tied into the sacramental life of the church, bound the individuals more closely into that life —at the baptism of their child, at marriage, and at death.

These then were the goals around which public and ecclesiastical policies were to be shaped. They were institutional goals. Later, we will explore the societal context in which they made sense. It is important to see them, however, as institutional, or official, goals. They functioned to shape policy. They could also be seen as goods to be achieved. It was only in the thirteenth century that people began to add companionship and love to the list of marital goods.

Motives

These purposes, however, were not always the reasons that individuals had for entering marriage, even though the church emphasized the importance of a free contract to secure these ends. The conscious reasons people would give for marrying might be economic security, status, acceptance by the community, romantic attachment, political power, and the like—beside or in addition to the official purposes of the marriage contract.[6] These reasons reflected the actual realities of power and desire in the particular situation.

The motives, the unconscious reasons bringing two people into

marriage, lie even deeper. These reflect conditions and dynamics
outside the calculating reason of the parties. Yet they have always
been extremely powerful forces affecting the outcome of our intentional enterprises, whether in love, battle, or business. Many of
them revolve around the drive to replicate our family of origin,
perhaps our most absolute world and the root of our convictions.
Or they may reflect a bitter fear of that world and a fantastic
attempt to escape it. We may be motivated to find a marriage in
which we can still be the child of our mother or father. We may be
driven to a particular partner by a need for victimage or victory.

Even the most resolute inspection of one's freedom to enter a
contract cannot discern all these motives. They form the preconditions of our life. Without them, however, we are like riders who
attempt a steeplechase without a horse. They give us the personal
power to approximate institutional goals. When they are compatible we find fulfillment in doing the expected. When they are not,
our lives become a torment of deviance.

These various purposes and motives are intricately intertwined
around the marital vine. They shape it and define the intersections
between the brick and mortar of institutions and the path of our
own growth. They add yet one more layer of complexity to the
interaction between church and marital institutions.

We have then a dynamic interchange formed by societal factors
(the four subjects) and ecclesial ones (the intentions of faith). Their
interchange is conditioned by the two functions of marriage (as
symbol of and *metaphor for* faith) as well as by institutional purposes and personal motives. To finish our framework for this complex interchange we must turn to the way these values are brought
together in key symbols and combined with social models that
shape our relationships in marriage and family life. It is in the
union of vibrant religious symbols and enduring patterns of social
relationships that we find viable resolutions to the argument
between faith and marriage.

NOTES

1. The function of symbols *of* and *for* reality receives its best-known
formulation by Clifford Geertz in "Religion as a Cultural System," in

Reader in Comparative Religion: An Anthropological Approach, ed. William A. Lessa and Evon Z. Vogt (2d ed.; New York: Harper & Row, 1965), 204–15.

2. Discussions of Paul's views on marriage and family are often mired in treatments of sexuality. For a start, see William E. Phipps, *Was Jesus Married? The Distortion of Sexuality in the Christian Tradition* (New York: Harper & Row, 1970), chap. 5. Kenneth Gangel surveys the epistles for a contemporary marital ethics in "Toward a Biblical Theology of Marriage and Family," *Journal of Psychology and Theology* 5:4 (Fall 1977): 318–31.

3. H. R. Niebuhr's classic treatment of the tension between church and society (*Christ and Culture* [New York: Harper & Brothers, 1954]) develops Ernst Troeltsch's distinction of church, sect, and mysticism into five more theologically grounded categories.

Eastern Orthodox thought on marriage offers some interesting alternatives for sacramentally oriented Western churches. Unfortunately I will not be able to take fuller account of them here. For a start, see Jean Meyendorff, *Marriage: An Orthodox Perspective* (Tuckahoe, N.Y.: St. Vladimir's Seminary Press, 1970).

The importance of marital and familial patterns for ecumenical relations can hardly be underestimated and deserves much more thorough discussion.

4. This understanding of faith receives a patient and penetrating treatment from a developmental perspective in James Fowler, *Stages of Faith* (New York: Harper & Row, 1981), though he does not make the distinction between being and will that I do.

5. This teleological approach to marriage arose first with St. Augustine. See his essays, "On the Good of Marriage," and "On Marriage and Concupiscence." This perspective was continued and amplified in later Thomistic literature. See Bernard Siegle, *Marriage Today: A Commentary on the Code of Canon Law* (3d rev. ed.; New York: Alba House, 1979), 29; and R. J. Levis, "Ends of Marriage," in *New Catholic Encyclopedia* (New York: McGraw-Hill, 1967) 9:267–70.

6. For recent research relating to mate selection, see John Gagnon and Cathy Greenblat, *Life Designs: Individuals, Marriages, and Families* (Glenview, Ill.: Scott, Foresman, 1978), 89–172; and Clyde and Susan Hendrick, *Liking, Loving, and Relating* (Monterey, Calif.: Brooks/Cole, 1983). Historical research has to be gleaned from personal papers, such as those in the fascinating collection by Donald M. Scott and Bernard Wishy, eds., *America's Families: A Documentary History* (New York: Harper & Row, 1982). For a statistical approach, see the essays by D. S. Smith and P. D. Hall in *The American Family in Socio-Historical Perspective*, ed. Michael Gordon (2d ed.; New York: St. Martin's Press, 1978).

3

Symbols
of Engagement

THE SYMBOLIC MODEL

We focus on symbols in this discussion because they are indispensable to the maintenance of any institutional pattern. Symbols are vivid images that condense many mental and emotional patterns into a unified perception. Symbols may be visual or aural. They often include taste, touch, and smell, as in the symbols of water, wine, and kiss. They bring together a publicly manifested value with deep personal bonds. The symbol of "fatherland," for instance, bonds people emotionally to a large collectivity and space by appealing to the most intimate bonds of their dependency. The institutions of married life are among the most stable in any society and also rely almost totally on learned compliance rather than outright coercion. Symbols are therefore crucial to their maintenance and also lead us to the dynamics inaugurating them.

Likewise, of course, faith life emerges in and gives rise to powerful and complex symbols. Faith is not merely a practical management of our affairs but a longing for perfection or fulfillment. Symbols take us beyond our present world even as they emerge from it. Bread becomes the Bread of Life. Wine becomes the Savior's redemptive blood. Symbolic life is central to faith and the dynamic of grace.

Symbols as such are highly diffuse. They bring together many different connotations and connections. They are condensations of multiple meanings that enable us to bind our lives to one another in complicated ways. In addition, symbols can gain more precise meaning for action by taking on particular *models*. A model is a pattern to emulate in behavior. "Fatherland" can take on the model of governance found in families dominated by fathers. The gathering of the twelve apostles around the Last Supper can become a model for governance by a group of elders.

Symbolic models stand at the junction of devotion and action.[1] They motivate us and also shape our patterns of action. The symbol "Body of Christ" not only calls on our loyalty to Jesus but also legitimates an organization in which our activities are functions to be coordinated by a head. "Free enterprise" not only exhorts us to exercise individual initiative but to do so in a marketplace constrained by the forces of supply and demand.

Symbols may take on and shed many different models in the course of time. People may share the same symbol but not the models of action they wear. The model of body identified with "Body of Christ" may shift from the organic one used above to a mechanical one, in which the members are interchangeable parts in a machine. "Free enterprise" may discard the model of the rural fair and identify with the market dominated by a few huge firms. Identification of these symbolic models and their use is one way of clarifying the interchange between Christianity and familial institutions.

This task requires two steps. First, we must identify the key symbols and models at work in Christian tradition. Then in subsequent chapters we will explore the various ways they have mediated the engagement between the four subjects of marriage and Christian faith. Only then can we construct an appropriate faith response to marriage in our own time and place.

THE CHRISTIAN SYMBOLS

The four most important symbols in the interchange have been sacrament, covenant, communion, and vocation. Others have played an important role. Trinity and friendship have highlighted some dimensions of communion. Discipleship and, more recently, pilgrimage have enriched vocation. Paschal mystery offers one way to entertain the symbol of sacrament, while contract—actually a model—has often attained symbolic status defining sacrament or covenant. The concept of marriage as forming a "domestic church" has also played an important role in shaping the nature and purpose of this sacramental or covenantal bond. Without attending to the specific meanings of each of these symbols or the models they have drawn on to inform marital life, let us get an idea of their general meaning.

Sacrament directs us first of all to the life of the church, especially its life of worship. Somehow the very life of Christ is palpably present in the actions of prayer, preaching, baptism, communion, confession, and priestly action. The symbol of sacrament disposes us to participation in these rituals as the means by which we nurture a life of faith.

Covenant brings to the fore the distinct parties in a relationship —God on the one hand, and the faithful respondents on the other. Covenants are promises predicated on the faithfulness of the covenanting persons. The source of the covenantal symbolism is the Bible rather than church ritual. It focuses on anticipation more than memory, discipline more than participation, a direct relationship with God more than life in the Body of Christ. It presents more of an ethical task than a ritual celebration.

With *communion* we tend to find a combination of these two. Communion connotes the intense participation of two persons in each other's life, bringing forth a unique community. It draws on the personal emphasis of covenant and the participatory nuance of sacrament, but subordinates their stress on God and church. It draws more on the natural forces uniting the unique persons, felt especially in their mutual bond. It draws our attention to their deep friendship as equal partners engaged in a common life.

Vocation draws on some of the biblical elements in covenant as well as the union of life in communion. It brings back the central role of God as the one who calls this couple into a particular kind of work, a particular form of holiness. In vocation, marriage draws us beyond our natural proclivities to a higher life of obedience to God's purposes for us and our world. Vocation orients us to the future and to a career of pursuing this unique work that God is leading us to.

Obviously, any symbol arising from the depths of faith or married life can become important in the interchange. These have gained a preeminence because they have sustained particular models guiding institutional practices. They tell us something about church and family just as they lead people to fulfill these behavioral expectations.

The subordinate symbols also have their potency, though perhaps they are not so widespread.[2] The Trinitarian relationship is often used to speak of the family, just as the family image (mother, father, child) is used to describe the Trinity, especially in simple catechisms. Here the loving devotion of the family members under the father's authority comes to the forefront of attention.

Marriage as a life of discipleship, found for instance in Elizabeth Achtemeier's work, emphasizes how the family is an arena in which to work out our faithful allegiance to Christ—his precepts, his example, his faith. The discipleship theme appears in a different way with the image of pilgrimage, in which the execution of precepts gives way to the incomplete and often erring wandering of the pilgrim. Here the goal is not clearly in view. One must deal with the struggles of the day with a dimmer understanding of the right path to follow. One lives more by hope and compassion than by achievement and moral will.

In the symbol of the paschal mystery we find an interpretation of sacrament that incorporates some of these pilgrimage themes. In this view our marital and familial life finds its essential meaning in the dynamics of death and resurrection manifested by Jesus Christ. Patterns of dying and rising are to be expected in marital life even as they assault us in our joy and retrieve us in our despair.

When it appears as a symbol, contract leads us to marriage as a set of reciprocal rights and duties. They are clear tasks requiring our presence as competent and mature persons. The parties need not be equal but their responsibilities are clearly set forth and publicly discernible. Marriage has clear boundaries and expectations. Marital life is the task of achieving them and calling each other to accountability.

Some of the implications for these differing symbols are already apparent. Even when we are not conscious of the symbols motivating and guiding our lives we can infer them from the characteristic dispositions and behaviors they evoke. Their implications are not automatic and fixed, however. The kinds of bonds they create among people depend on the models they take on in various circumstances.

THE MODELS

There have been essentially three models for defining the structure of marriage and family—hierarchical, organic, and egalitarian.[3] When we speak of a model we turn our attention to the pattern of relationships among the parents, children, relatives, and household members. What is the structure in which they house their motives, purposes, faith, and personalities?

The most widespread model has been that of a hierarchy of authority. It has been almost exclusively a patriarchal form. Like a great chain of being, the family devolves from the father to the mother, and from them to the male and female children, with the slaves and animals of the household bringing up the rear. We find this model in St. Paul's letters (1 Cor. 11:3-9), in many Christian traditions, and in recent Catholic and Protestant teaching. It is a model emphasizing authority, obedience, service, and patient submission. For the male it also includes the call to courage, charity, and noblesse oblige.

When the reciprocal obligations of the husband and wife are emphasized, we move in the direction of an organic model. Here we move away from the hierarchy of command to the organic interdependence of function. Each role has certain functions to play that the others cannot. The man must give overall guidance and relate the family to the wider world. The woman must have babies and run the household (which may include an extensive agricultural operation). The children each have chores appropriate to their gender and age. Power is dispersed according to function. While the father generally retains an overall authority, it is conditioned by the realities of interdependence, which gives each person an authority in his or her sphere. We find this model in St. Paul (1 Corinthians 7) as well as in various strands of Christian tradition to the present day.

The organic and hierarchical models should not be confused. The rights that inhere almost exclusively in the father in the hierarchical model are distributed to the members in the organic one. The family as such has its own status rather than being simply the extension of the father's will. The classic niche for this model is agricultural, but towns and cities have also been congenial to this model among artisans and small family businesses. Here the family is actually ruled by the necessities of maintaining the estate, farm, or enterprise. Each member has a power and dignity arising from his or her function. In the hierarchical model obedience is stressed; in the organic, cooperation. Unless we see this distinction we cannot detect when one model is invoked to disguise the actual employment of the other. For instance, people will often use organic symbolism to mask over the actualities of command and subordination.

The egalitarian model stresses equality and partnership between husband and wife, extending a kind of potential friendship even to the children, as when parents and children are on a first-name basis. In this model the spouses are primarily friends. They are roughly equal in power and share authority for all major decisions. They value intimacy over submission, role sharing over functional distinctions. In this model marriage appears as a distinctive kind of friendship.[4]

While we find evidences of this relationship in the Bible, especially Genesis 2, the Song of Songs, and other writings, it is hardly a New Testament idea. Friendship between the sexes was practically unheard of in classical culture. Since women and men were considered inherently unequal, and certainly were unequal in social power, the peculiar equality of friendship was impossible for them. The most they could strive for would be a hierarchical or organic model exercised with charity.

The implications of attributing souls to both men and women, the sanctification of womanhood through the cult of the Virgin Mary, and the equality of status achieved in baptism and mystical experience, however, all worked slowly but inevitably to raise up the notion that Christian marriage was a friendship between equals. We find this in the writings of Martin Luther and in Puritan authors such as John Milton.[5] In our own time this theme has become increasingly pronounced in society as well as in the church.

The three models form a kind of spectrum, with the hierarchical at one end stressing a pyramid of authority and the egalitarian on the other emphasizing the equality between friends. The organic conception occupies a distinct middle ground and has its own social niche, especially in stable agrarian cultures where the household is a productive economic unit. The hierarchical model, with its military subordination, can be characteristic of times of rapid change and uncertainty as well as of cultures with a sharp distinction of public and private worlds. The egalitarian model rests on women gaining a relative control over their power of reproduction and production. It is characteristic of situations where family members must share the power they derive from participation in other institutions.

The various symbols we cited earlier can be bound to these models in greater or lesser degree. The symbol of sacrament, for instance, has been attached to all three, while communion tends to identify strongly with the egalitarian model. All of these combinations reflect changing social circumstances affecting the exercise of male and female roles. Finally, these symbolic models can have a variable relation to the four subjects of marriage—the persons, the couple, the family, and the household. Failure to recognize the complex relationships of symbols, models, and subjects obscures our vision of the richness and confusion characterizing the interplay between Christian faith and marital reality. This interplay can now be laid out in its formal complexity.

NOTES

1. This variable relationship between symbol and model is dealt with as the tension among loyalty, theory, and practice in Everett and Bachmeyer's *Disciplines in Transformation* (see chap. 1 n. 10). See my earlier essay, "Cybernetics and Symbolic Body Model," *Zygon* 7.2 (June 1972):98–109.

2. Bernard Häring's earlier work, *Marriage in the Modern World*, trans. G. Stevens (Westminster, Md.: Newman Press, 1965), esp. 88–134, uses the Trinity. Later, in "The Christian Family as a Community of Salvation: A Theoretical View," in Karl Rahner et al.'s *Man Before God* (New York: P. J. Kenedy & Sons, 1966), 146–58, he took up the concept of "saving community," which then influenced the treatment at Vati-

can II in the Pastoral Declaration, *The Church in the Modern World (Gaudium et Spes)*, chap. 47.

Elizabeth Achtemeier, in *The Committed Marriage* (Philadelphia: Westminster Press, 1976), uses the symbol of discipleship with an egalitarian accent. Stephen B. Clark expresses discipleship in a subordinationist model in *Man and Woman in Christ: A Study of the Roles of Men and Women in the Light of Scripture and the Social Sciences* (Ann Arbor, Mich.: Servant, 1980). Both authors appeal to God's purposes and will—familiar themes in the general concept of vocation.

The Holy Family as an ideal for marriage goes back to St. Francis and is widespread in popular Catholicism, especially in French Canada, where the Holy Family holds a preeminent position as an exemplar of virtue for men, women, and children. See X. D. Macleod's *History of the Devotion to the Blessed Virgin Mary in North America* (Baltimore: John B. Piet, 1882), 127–30.

The idea of marriage as a contract occurs not only in Roman canon law and civil law but also in secular philosophy, as with Immanuel Kant: "Matrimony is an agreement between two persons by which they grant each other equal reciprocal rights, each of them undertaking to surrender the whole of the person to the other with a complete right of disposal over it. . . . In this way the two persons become a unity of will" (*Lectures on Ethics*, trans. Louis Infield [New York: Harper & Row, 1963] 167).

The marriage contract (*ketubah*) so central in Judaism is rooted not so much in covenant as in commercial transaction. See Louis M. Epstein, *The Jewish Marriage Contract: A Study in the Status of the Woman in Jewish Law* (New York: Arno Press, [1927] 1973), chap. 1.

The Roman Catholic situation is summarized by William Bassett in "The Marriage of Christians: Valid Contract, Valid Sacrament?" in *The Bond of Marriage: An Ecumenical and Interdisciplinary Study*, ed. William Bassett (Notre Dame, Ind.: University of Notre Dame Press, 1968), 117–80.

3. The hierarchical model is well known in feminist literature, where it has been critiqued thoroughly in its sexual as well as religious dimensions. See Kari E. Børreson, *Subordination and Equivalence: The Nature and Role of Women in Augustine and Thomas Aquinas* (Washington, D.C.: University Press of America, 1981), and Carol Ochs, *Behind the Sex of God: Toward a New Consciousness—Transcending Matriarchy and Patriarchy* (Boston: Beacon Press, 1977). David Bakan picks up the biblical origins in psychological perspective in *And They Took Themselves Wives: The Emergence of Patriarchy in Western Society* (New York: Harper & Row, 1979). Steven Goldberg reiterates patriarchal claims in *The Inevitability of Patriarchy: Why the Biological Difference Between Men and Women Always Produces Male Domination* (New York: William Morrow, 1973).

Ivan Illich points out some of the significance of the less-obvious organic model in *Gender* (New York: Pantheon Books, 1982). This functionalist model, however, is much better known behind the systems theories of the family (see chap. 6 n. 7).

For egalitarian models, see Alice S. Rossi, "Sex Equality: The Beginnings of Ideology," in *Confronting the Issues: Sex Roles, Marriage, and the Family,* ed. Kenneth C. W. Kammeyer (Boston: Allyn & Bacon, 1975), 364–76; Benjamin R. Barber, *Liberating Feminism* (New York: Seabury Press, 1975); and for a fresh look at Christian origins, Elizabeth Schüssler Fiorenza, *In Memory of Her: A Feminist Theological Reconstruction of Christian Origins* (New York: Crossroad, 1983).

4. Ancient authors did acknowledge a kind of friendship among unequals, but its real heart was always to be seen in the relationship between equals. See Jeffrey Blustein, *Parents and Children: The Ethics of the Family* (New York and London: Oxford University Press, 1982).

Friendship, not surprisingly, is an increasingly widespread interest among scholars. For a theological reflection, see Gilbert Meilander, *Friendship: A Study in Theological Ethics* (Notre Dame, Ind.: University of Notre Dame Press, 1980). Rosemary Rader explores the phenomenon in the early church in *Breaking Boundaries: Male/Female Friendship in Early Christian Communities* (Ramsey, N.J.: Paulist Press, 1983). See also Leon Morris, *Testaments of Love: A Study of Love in the Bible* (Grand Rapids: Wm. B. Eerdmans, 1981). For Luther's views and some contemporary reflections, read Gerta Scharffenorth, "Freunde in Christus," in Gerta Scharffenorth and Klaus Thraede, *"Freunde in Christus Werden . . ."* (Gelnhausen and Berlin: Burckhardthaus Verlag, 1977), esp. 233–35, 281–83. The idea of the conpanionate marriage received its modern impetus with the path-breaking book by Ben B. Lindsey and Wainwright Evans, *The Companionate Marriage* (New York: Boni & Liveright, 1927). For a contemporary sensitive treatment, see Warren L. Moulton, *Friends, Partners, and Lovers* (Valley Forge, Pa.: Judson Press, 1979).

5. The Puritans, contrary to popular myth, were early proponents of marriage as a kind of friendship. Though John Milton's defense of divorce on the basis of incompatibility was more radical than most Puritans, he only expressed the direction things were taking. John Halkett presents an incisive analysis in *Milton and the Idea of Matrimony: A Study of the Divorce Tracts and "Paradise Lost"* (New Haven, Conn.: Yale University Press, 1970). Edmund Leites provides a mine of insights in "The Duty to Desire: Love, Friendship, and Sexuality in Some Puritan Theories of Marriage," *Comparative Civilizations Review* 3 (Fall 1979): 40–82. See also Robert R. Bell, *Marriage and Family Interaction* (3d ed.; Homewood, Ill.: Dorsey Press, 1971), chap. 2.

4

Symbolic Models
in Transition

The meaning of marriage has undergone a change in sociological *subject*, relational *model*, and theological *symbol*. We have already seen how the focus of marriage has shifted from the household to the couple and person. Marriage is increasingly seen less as a mode of householding or as the core of family than as a peculiar bond between two persons, which makes them into a couple. This is not only a shift in people's personal motives for entering into marriage. Even more important, our institutions—the church, law, and culture—see their purposes carried out through a personal approach to marriage. This is not to say that the other subjects, such as household and family, are now missing. It is merely to say that marriage is not automatically focused on them.

We have also observed that the dominant model for marriage has changed from that of hierarchy and organism to that of equality. The pattern of relationships in marriage is not characterized by control and subordination, but by mutuality and equality. We are concerned more with developing the power of the persons in their relationship than in adhering to a received pattern of authority. This again is not only a matter of people's motives for entering marriage, but also of the way laws, churches, and our culture shape our expectations about married life. It is also the way our laws increasingly handle the issues of property and parenting, whether through provision for community property, child custody, or tax liability.

Shifts among the four key Christian symbols have not been as pronounced, but are still noticeable. Taking the longer view, we can see that marriage as sacrament came into dominance in the Western church after Augustine, reaching its crystallization by the thirteenth century. With the Protestant Reformation the symbol of sacrament was offset by the rise of covenantal and vocational symbols for marriage. The church focus underscored by sacrament shifted to a focus on the partners' personal relationship with God. Marriage was seen more purely as an ethical matter to be controlled by government than a symbolic matter to be controlled by a church.

In recent years Catholics and Protestants have begun correcting each other's one-sided emphases. Catholics began to appropriate vocational and covenantal symbolism at Vatican II and in subsequent theological discussion. Protestants were more willing to reopen the question of marriage's sacramentality. Both traditions, however, began to shift toward an embrace of communion as a central symbol for marriage. While this is due in major part to the rising social emphasis on personality, equality, and friendship, it is also due to a renewed appreciation of the richness of Christian approaches to marriage. This greater historical sense has made it possible to relativize the preoccupation with sacrament, covenant, and vocation that had dominated Christian approaches in the past.

Nevertheless, Christians have not experienced a headlong embrace of communion as their preferred symbol. Important branches of Christianity still invoke the other symbols, often with renewed vigor. There are important reactions against equality, personhood, and communion, both in established denominations and in newer movements.

We will approach the complexity of these transitions by focusing on changes in the meaning of the four key symbols—sacrament, covenant, vocation, and communion. In each case we will explore the way the shift from household to person and from hierarchy to equality has affected the meaning of the symbol. With each symbol we will see how important countertrends exist seeking to uphold the model of hierarchical household in the face of egalitarian personhood.

The purpose of this complicated undertaking is to understand the alternatives facing people who want to approach marriage in terms of Christian faith. Each combination has its own constellation of psychological patterns, social context, and faith commitment. We need to see what key values are being upheld in each case, values calling for our profound consideration in any effort to construct our own approaches in our contemporary situations.

MARRIAGE AS SACRAMENT

"Sacrament" connotes participation in the symbolic life of the church. The bond this creates with the church is not so much one of obedience to norms as it is reinforcement of structures of authority. It is not as concerned with ethical consequences as it is with the grounding of social and ecclesial institutions in the basic structure of life—especially of life as lived in faith. It emphasizes that God's grace works through nature rather than through an imposed order. Therefore we would expect sacramental approaches to be more authoritarian but less legalistic, more concerned with integrity of symbol than with the justice of relationships. How then do these concerns work out in the framework of subjects and models?[1]

If we lay out the models and subjects in terms of a table, we find a following constellation of sacramental forms (see page 38).

As we can see, sacramental symbolism clusters in the corner of "hierarchical household." The idea that the family is to form a household that will be a "little church" is a longstanding one, perhaps of Jewish origin. St. Paul speaks of "households of faith," making the domestic symbol a symbol for faith. We find a more organic representation of this view in his Corinthian and Colossian letters, a more hierarchical one in Ephesians. Recently we find Pope John Paul II lifting up this model in his exhortation, *Consortio Familiaris*. Here marriage and family are ultimately a form of participation in and service to the life of the church. Not only are they to be a model of the church's structure, as in Ephesians, but also a vehicle for the church's public mission. They are to be in miniature a place of hospitality, public service, charity, and refuge.

Here we find an important value. Faith requires that marriage lead back out into a wider world. The private and intimate realities

Model

Subject	Hierarchy	Organism	Equality
Person	Paschal mystery		Paschal pilgrimage
Couple	*Mysterion* of St. Paul (Eph.) "Little church" (John Paul II)	"Holy family"	Encounter (Schillebeeckx)
Family			
Household	Faith community (St. Paul [Cor.])		School of faith

must evince a drive toward public life and service. Love must finally manifest its significance. It must symbolize its inner life in a way the world can know and understand. In giving witness to its heart it strengthens others and draws them closer to that possibility for their lives. Simultaneously creation of a worldly household structure gives the partners an enduring frame of reference that continually re-creates their relation. It gives a common structure to awaken them from an aimless drifting in which they will forget their central concerns and lose their bearings. The household offers protection and refuge as well as a means for proclaiming the couple's good news to the world. In short, love has a drive for publicity and expression. Christian life must support that drive and give it shape. This is the central value of the sacramental household.

The weakness of this symbolic model is its neglect of the very love that seeks publicity and structure. It places a great emphasis on the expectations of the church and less on the natural dynamics of love. The institution of marriage takes precedence over the emotional bond of two married people. In doing so institutional concerns for order, durability, and permanence come to shape the theological meaning. Sacrament comes to legitimate institutional concerns of householding over personal concerns for emotional communion.

In assuming that nature is already "graced" sacramental approaches begin to expect too much of ordinary marriages. To the degree that grace is identified with church interests and activities, it begins to place too many institutional demands on ordinary people. While claiming the abundant presence of redemption, it cannot mediate forgiveness, because it denies the personal reality of brokenness, corruption, and perversity in our life. In being concerned primarily for institutional matters of householding and family, it can claim that "marriage" survives even though particular marriages do not. In the end a sacramental symbol can be an ideology for church control and a reduction of married life to institutional form.

In the symbolism of the Holy family we find a less institutional form that precedes the church, just as Christmas precedes Pentecost. It begins with Jesus' family rather than the settled forms of church worship. Here we find the family as a model of the divine relationship itself, not just of Christ's union with the church. Household structure gives way to emotional bond and organic interplay as dominant themes.

This marital model does not yet come to focus on the couple, however. It is the *child* that bonds the parents together. They are related to each other through the child. It is as family that they are husband and wife. Mary's virginity emphasizes that it is not their sexual bond but their parenthood that marries them to each other. Moreover, their existence is not for the sake of themselves or their family, but for the sake of being an instrument of God's revelation. The family of faith is a means for God's working in the world.

More recently, in the work of Edward Schillebeeckx, we see the symbol of sacrament used to speak of the encounter of persons with Christ and of Christ with God. The interpersonal model of encounter interprets sacrament, providing the basis for a theory of marriage as a sacrament of encounter. Sacrament is not reduced to the dynamics of the couple. Their life as a couple is still a means for being related to God through Christ. The concerns of household and family drop away, however, in the face of the overriding intent to form a personal relation with God. From that core one can move out to family, society, and church.

In general we see a trend from the hierarchical household to personal equality, from "little church" to "encounter." It is attenuated at the personal level, to be sure. Important counterthrusts exist in order to maintain certain ecclesial values. Moreover, some options tend to be neglected. Distinctive motifs—of participation in the ecclesial life of Christ, and of being a manifestation of divine redemption—are maintained, but with different meanings for our life.

Finally, we must take note of imaginative ways that the two dominant poles can be reconciled by turning to the notion of paschal mystery and school of faith. In seeing marriage as a paschal mystery, we emphasize the way marital life participates in the dying and rising of Christ. When cast into a hierarchical model, it emphasizes the way we live sacrificially to God. In its more egalitarian form it sees our participation more in terms of walking with Jesus in his pilgrimage than in the mystery of his dying and rising.

This symbol helps us make sense of the sorrow, joy, loss, and reward that we experience. It also calls into question any superficial hedonism or morbid despair. It stresses the way that sacrifice is more than the sacrifice of subordination and noblesse oblige between husband and wife, and between parent and child. It is a reciprocal dynamic buried deeply within our own individual efforts at survival, expression, beauty, and meaning. Finally, the paschal symbol is a very personal one giving meaning to our lives even in the destruction of our marriages by death and divorce. Through it we find another way of seeing marriage as participation in the life of Christ.

Similarly, when we wish to stress equality without losing the sense of household, we can speak of marriage as a school for faith. It is not merely a matter of parents instructing children. It is a matter of seeing how each life in the household can be a means of revelation to the others. The infant is as much a clue to divine love as the grandparent, the guest and stranger as much as the spouse. Marriage creates a framework for learning faith, not just with our heads but with our hearts, not only rationally but also symbolically. As a household of equality it is a way of learning God in child and stranger. It manifests Christ as the Teacher of the world.

These are only a few ways that sacramental symbolism can find meaning in different models of family and with differing subjects as its focus. While the central values of participation in the life of Christ and openness to church and society persist, they take on differing forms and meanings. Though they all see God's grace transforming our nature, they construe this nature differently, either for theological, psychological, or sociological reasons.

As we have seen, the emphasis on household leads us to see marriage as a vehicle not merely of sacrifice but of service, not merely of churchliness but of worldliness. When these values are stressed even more strongly we begin to pick up the symbol of vocation. This central symbol has its own unique story of transition to tell.

MARRIAGE AS VOCATION

When marriage is seen as a vocation, it is lived as a response to some purpose beyond its nature. It begins more with God's gracious call than with the order of creation. It is an instrument in carrying out God's plan, a vehicle for God's purposes. It becomes a way of "building the kingdom," "renewing the earth," or advancing human progress. As Elizabeth Achtemeier puts it, it is a work of discipleship. Marital life is a way of responding to God's call.[2]

The meaning of vocation has shifted dramatically in Western Christianity. In early medieval times, Christians developed an increasingly individualized notion of vocation, which further stimulated the differentiation of persons from marriage, family, and household. The call to be a holy people, which had been delivered first to Israel and then to the church, was transmuted into a personal call for each saint. Finally it became intensified as a way of life for the few—the monks and nuns. Once it had become condensed in this sense of personal career it could then be released again into the world in a secular form. The call to the holy life became the motivation to pursue a career or occupation. It came to legitimate the lowliest of worldly economic concerns. In our own time the immense economic structure this has reinforced has provided the material basis for the individualized personalization we observed earlier.

Not only has vocation's meaning for marriage changed over

time but it also exhibits a great plurality of forms in our own time. By resorting again to our table of subjects and models we can map out some of these meanings.

Model

Subject	Hierarchy	Organism	Equality
Person	Heroic faith (Kierkegaard, Hauerwas)	Cosmos of callings S. Clark	Discipleship (Achtemeier)
Couple		Missionary Couples K. Barth *Gaudium et Spes*	
Family		Christian Family Movement	
Household	Unification Church (Moon)		Worker/ consumer household

Here we have almost a bewildering set of options. The pattern instituted by Rev. Sun Myung Moon for the Unification Church focuses mainly on the family as the point of recovery of the three blessings humanity lost in the Fall. All the resources of the household tend to be drawn into this response to God's calling to this new creation. Marriages are approved by Rev. Moon to advance the regeneration of the human race. His own second marriage is the fount of this regeneration. The families instituted by his decisions exist not at all for the purposes of the parties but for this divine call. So important is this higher call that the partners rarely consummate their bond before a set period of service for the church.

In this case marriage as a process of nature is clearly subordinated to the grace that comes through response to God's call to renew the creation. When a more cooperative stance is taken toward creation we find a more organic model that gives more attention to the initiative of the couple. This pattern was widespread among Catholics in the Christian Family Movement in the post-World War II period as well as in the document *Gaudium et Spes (The Church in the Modern World)* at Vatican II. Here marriage is a vocation to build up the world and to advance the kingdom of God. It has a high instrumental quality as a valid and important vehicle of response to God's call—a call not restricted to priests and religious. Structurally, it tended to remain hierarchical or organic.

Karl Barth's presentation of marriage, though acknowledging the trinitarian model for interpersonal encounter, rests on vocation and command, and utilizes an organic model of male "dignity in succession." Marriage is "a supremely particular vocation" in which the man exercises leadership and the woman faithfully cooperates in accord with God's creative will.

When this vocational sense is carried into a personal and egalitarian framework we have the conception of marriage as a form of discipleship. It is a way that people try to carry out the call they receive from God. Their equality springs from their call to discipleship rather than from their nature. Discipleship creates an equality of servanthood in place of the natural hierarchies of domestic duty. As Elizabeth Achtemeier points out, the relationship to God stands prior to the marital life and gives it direction, purpose, and meaning.

When vocation is interpreted in personal terms, marriage can be a pursuit of some *goal,* as with Achtemeier, or it can be the possession of a *status,* as with Barth. In some late medieval conceptions there was a "cosmos of callings" occupied by persons. The cosmos itself took care of the functional needs of the world. People's concern was not to pursue particular goals and change it, but to fulfill faithfully the roles in it. In our own time this sense leads people to see in the marital vocation the fulfillment of certain gender-based roles—the man as father and breadwinner, the woman as mother and housewife. This seems to be the orientation taken by Stephen Clark in obedience to models drawn from Scripture and corroborated, he believes, by contemporary social science.

When the immediate relationship to God comes to the fore, vocation as status and as pursuit of a goal merge in the idea of marriage as a heroic act of obedience to God. This seems to be the direction taken by Kierkegaard and also seems to underlie the position advanced by Stanley Hauerwas. Marriage is a state of life or arena of action in which one cultivates the virtues and character God calls us to manifest—patience, humility, self-sacrifice, and generativity. This is a highly individualistic conception in which the nature of the persons is subordinated to their potential for grace. But this individualism is far from the interpersonal values we find in the symbol of communion. It is also quite far from the last, more secularized, manifestation of vocation displayed in our table.

In North Atlantic middle-class society adults and children are recognized as dutiful consumers and producers. With regard to the economy they are all equal in importance. Even at an early age people gain a certain economic independence from the household by which they pursue their own interests. This is the egalitarian household in service to the structure of occupations and markets. It is quite clearly the secularized outcome of a long process of devolution in the concept of vocation. I have listed it here to alert us to its actual prominence in the lives of contemporary Christians. To the extent that we construe vocation in terms of career, economy, and personal life goals, we "buy into" this influential model of family life.

The conception of marriage as vocation centers around response to God's call as an order brought to or imposed upon our natural life. Grace supercedes nature. It is, however, still a call and not a command. Our life is a response and not a knuckling under. The more we press the dialogical character of this call the more we move toward a conception of marriage as a covenant in which the parties interact in accord with a system of promises among them. Here again we find a multiplicity of forms this theological symbol can take.

MARRIAGE AS COVENANT

While the symbol of covenant is very widespread in the Bible its application to marriage comes later. Biblical covenant contains both hierarchical as well as egalitarian and organic features.[3] It appears hierarchically in the suzerainty covenants discussed by

Mendenhall. It takes an egalitarian form as the basis for the relationship among the twelve tribes of Israel. Covenant may have a conditional quality, as in Deuteronomy, or a permanent and unconditional one, as in the Davidic covenant. In the first, the preservation of the covenant rests on the mutual performance of duties. In the second, it rests on the irrevocable intentions of God. Sometimes the covenant is manifested in the very impersonal forms of law and command, as with the covenant at Sinai. In other places it is a very intimate relationship of love, as in Hosea's depiction of Yahweh's parental relationship to Israel.

Covenant has always had an ambiguous relationship to contract. While sometimes they have simply been equated, we must keep them distinct in our minds. Contract in itself has always implied some kind of legal equality, whereas covenant, *foedus*, has always had some quality of being imposed or offered by a higher party. While some biblical covenants were among equals, it is the egalitarian thrust contained in the Roman notion of contract that has led to our contemporary understanding of marital covenant. Of course, earlier concepts of the marriage contract were still overpowered by the hierarchical way it was an imposed contract into which the parties entered. The entry was supposed to be voluntary, the contract was not.

All of these themes are carried over into the various covenantal conceptions of marriage.[4] Even though this marital symbol is very widespread, its forms seem to fall along a fairly narrow range of options. Some of its more unusual forms are generally handled better by the other symbols. Turning to our table we can see this fairly clearly (see page 46).

When covenant is interpreted in a hierarchical structure it points to the way marriage creates an analogue of the divine-human relation, or of the relation between Christ and the church. This covenantal structure is not merely imposed on nature, in the way of obedience, but is a new order, a new nature. The covenanted community that this creates tends to be set apart. This is clearly manifested in the Mennonite or Amish pattern in which the entire household with its attendant economy exists in relative separation from the world. With charismatic communities, such as those that grew up in the 1960s in Ann Arbor and elsewhere, these

Model

Subject	Hierarchy	Organism	Equality
Person	Puritan duty of covenant (Adams)		Androgynous plurality (W. Yates)
Couple		Charismatic Communities	(P. Palmer)
Family	Latter-day Saints	*Gaudium et Spes* P.E.T. (E. Gaulke)	
Household	Mennonites		"Little commonwealth"

covenanted communities have a more selective detachment and do not set up entirely separate economies. Attention rests more on the family's covenant than on the household's.

The Church of Jesus Christ of Latter-day Saints, usually called the Mormons, reflects another variant of this pattern. Mormon theology is highly covenantal and emphasizes the primacy of the whole church as the object of God's covenant with the saints gathered for the perfection of creation. The Mormon experiment with polygamous marriages in the nineteenth century resulted from a direct claim of Joseph Smith's. Its main theological function seems to have been to establish the eternity and equal validity of all God's covenants with the Saints, even those from Israel's patriarchal times. In fact, Mormon practice reflects a curious tension. Women are accorded a great deal of equality in the public realm, while functioning in an organic or hierarchical manner in the family, whose structure mirrors the church's priestly order. The covenantal order of the church is reflected in the family, rather than the family being an instrument of mission, as it is in vocational models.

In all these cases covenantal models direct people as much to the relationships among them as to the God who establishes covenant with and through them. Vocational models stress the immediate responsibilities of the subjects to God rather than this structure of relationships. Herein lies one of the most important differences between the two symbols. Vocation draws us to a goal, covenant to a pattern of relationships.

As we move away from a household and community focus we pick up themes found also in Vatican II's *Gaudium et Spes*. Here covenant becomes a way of speaking of organic mutuality without recourse to a theory of nature. Instead it emphasizes the gracious promises of God and our free response. The concern for an instrumental vision of family manifested in vocation is harmonized with the symbolic expression of divine love in sacrament.

In contemporary Protestantism the covenant model is very widespread. For some it is a protest against the overly mechanistic and individualistic connotations of contract. For others it is a correction of the overly naturalistic approaches in organic models of sacrament or of over-institutionalization in hierarchical sacramental models.

When the family is the focus we find the adoption of contractualist exchange theory, as in the work of Earl Gaulke who draws on Parent Effectiveness Training. The family becomes an elaborate pattern of explicit negotiation among all its members. For many people this forms a bridge between the deep and permanent stabilities of family life and the constant renegotiation typical of mercantile society. It is in this sense conditioned by middle-class values and can easily be absorbed by an entirely secular view that forgets how it is tied into the divine dialogue with us.

One of the typical features of covenantal theories, one they share to some extent with vocational ones, is their focus on will and intention rather than nature and inherited disposition. The actors and the powers they bring to the covenantal drama are very important. Whereas sacramental symbols tend to emphasize conformation to a structure of true authority, covenant stresses the exercise of power in creating a new world.

This characteristic becomes quite prominent when the subjects of marriage are the couple and persons. Here the contractualist element becomes even more acute. In the work of John Scanzoni marriage emerges as a delicate structure of negotiations resting on the powers of the persons involved. When this negotiation expresses an underlying covenant of love, marriage will be viable. When it does not, and when the power imbalance is too great, it will often shatter.

A very different approach to covenant is taken by Paul Palmer in his earlier work. Here covenant is being used to undercut the more impersonal contractualism found in earlier Catholic practice. Covenant connotes an intimate personal bond (the Hosea view) that demands flexible response between the partners.

As Palmer later seems to have realized, this usage was a little confused. Covenant was employed to combat the implications of a sacramental approach that put church requirement above marital creativity. The real issue, however, was the movement from hierarchical to egalitarian marital modes. By indirectly undercutting those hierarchical and organic sacramental models he moved Catholic thought closer to the kind of contractualism espoused by Scanzoni. In the end his underlying theological values moved him toward the communion symbol we will explore last.

Finally, when covenant is pressed in a very personalistic and egalitarian direction it can be used to advance an almost androgynous mutuality, as in Wilson Yates's position. Here we find both a kind of organicism and sheer equality. Not only are the parties able to exchange roles, they are able to re-create them in a variety of ways. There is the attention to functionality typical of the organic model as well as to equality of power. In the mutual participation in a great variety of roles each person touches more deeply on the ultimate meaning of love in this world. Sometimes these roles can be highly familial, sometimes they are limited to the couple alone. Thus, the androgynous model, as Yates points out, is a highly pluralistic one. In drawing on interior creative powers of the persons and promoting a wide-ranging mutuality it borders on the communion model.

Covenant models of a personal-hierarchical or a household-egalitarian type are less widespread. Marriage as the outcome of a personal covenant with God seems to lie behind the Puritan model illuminated by Edmund Leites. As an example of Puritan theology consider this representative passage from Richard Adams [1683]:

The wife hath plighted her troth to her husband according to the
flesh, unto whom the Lord hath in the marriage-covenant joined her;
and she is obliged to be constantly faithful in all conjugal duties to
him with whom she hath trusted herself, and that by virtue of the
covenant of her God.

More immediately, the Puritans saw this covenant as an ordi-
nance of mutual rights and duties. Here, people engage in marriage and maintain it out of a covenantal obligation with God.
Even their cultivation of interpersonal desire arises as an expression of their individual covenants with God. This is a marriage
resulting from the religious virtues of the individuals. The actual
hierarchy of the marriage prevents them from immediate friendship, but their duty to God obligates them to sustain the marriage
as if friendship actually existed. This, as Leites points out, is a difficult task. The personal covenant with a superior God is very hard
to sustain in marriage.

Similarly, a household of covenanting members has difficulty
taking account of children. We can, of course, see children as having an implicit covenant of consent. They are to be treated as citizens of the covenanting community as soon as possible—their
deviant behavior curbed at an early age and their capacity for
rational debate and decision making encouraged as soon as possible. Everyone has definite duties to perform, though these are
renegotiated as the child grows older. Perhaps the best example of
this approach arose with the Puritan claim that the family was a
"little commonwealth." The family was molded around a civic
ideal for which the members were to be trained through family disciplines. In its modern form, rooted in bourgeois culture, it is
found in the parent-effectiveness model advanced by Gaulke.

The covenant symbol draws us to a new community, a new
nature of relationships within the world. It is rich with the dialogue
sought so frequently in marriages and families today. Its strength
lies in the way it combines commitment and relationship. Its weakness, however, lies in its tendency to leave the natural energies of
people behind for the sake of a lofty ideal that can become a dead-
ening structure of obligation and exterior transactions. Those who
seek in the covenant of marriage a vibrant and energizing love
press beyond this symbol to that of communion.

MARRIAGE AS COMMUNION

The more that covenant becomes a free flow of response between persons, the closer we get to the symbol of communion.
With communion we stress the resonance of two natures, the
mutual participation in what is common to the persons involved.
This is not merely a participation in some world they hold in common. It is participation in the qualities they each have as persons.
Marriage is not so much a product of their moral wills and intentions as it is the manifestation of their inherent likeness.

As we stress this inherent similarity and mutuality we narrow
this communion to the spouses themselves, for only they can share
in the equality of power necessary to maintain this process of reciprocal response. Children can share this only to a limited degree
because their repertoire of psychological skills is not sufficiently
developed. Communion rests on equality of power, not on obedience to a transcendent pattern.

The symbol of communion seems to have its religious origin in
mystical experience. It is a symbolization of ecstasy. It is a marital
symbol rooted in immediate experience of God or the godhead,
rather than biblical history (covenant), church order (sacrament),
or divine mission (vocation).

In communion, therefore, we see grace operating through nature
—that is, through the given structures of personality characteristic
of the individuals involved. In taking nature seriously, communion
stands close to sacrament, but lacks the external or permanent
symbolic structure typical of sacrament. Communion rests on the
intimate and emotional correspondence of the persons. Sacrament,
with its symbolic clarity, ongoing structure, and church context, is
oriented more to institutional authority. Because sacrament has
tended to emphasize that grace is *redemptive*, however, it raises
nature to a new level rather than simply working through nature.
Therefore, it tends to bind marriages more closely to the institutional church. Communion, by focusing on the peculiar natures of
the persons, is more loosely attached to given institutions.
Moreover, because it sees grace as a creative process arising
through nature, it is less likely to stress the way the church trans-
forms that nature. This is why communion models, as we shall see,

view marriage as a metaphor *for* faith rather than as a symbolic manifestation *of* faith.

This is not to say, however, that we do not find some interpretations of communion manifesting hierarchical models or being tied to family and household. To see the significance of such interpretations, let us turn to our table for the last time.[5]

Model

Subject	Hierarchy	Organism	Equality
Person	Ascetic mystics		E. & J. Whitehead
			J. Nelson
Couple			J. Nilson
			C. van der Poel
Family		*Gaudium et Spes,* Chap. 47	
	Trinity (B. Häring)		
Household			

While we can see that communion presses toward a sense of equality in power, its traditional public formulation has expressed some sense of hierarchy—in the personal case, between God and the self, in the familial case, the precedence of the father over the mother and child. In Bernard Häring's earlier work we find a clear expression of the Trinitarian communion applied to the family.

For Häring the Trinity connotes a profound interpenetration among the three persons, yet still within some kind of hierarchy. The Trinity expresses the emotional reality of the patriarchal family. The Father has precedence. He is the principle of creation, governance, and power. From the Father comes the Son—the heir of the Father. The Spirit, the feminine principle, makes this possible. Here we can see the legitimating symbol of patriarchy, primogeniture, and self-effacing femininity.

The primary unit is not the Father, the Son, or the Spirit, however. It is the godhead. Sociologically, it is the family or household community. It is the *patrimonium* that is to be maintained and transmitted. All the members participate in this community of goods, though in different ways. Moreover, the father's control as well as the powers of the son and mother rely more on emotional control than on external exercise of power. With the Trinity we find a symbolization of marriage that partakes much more of the psychological dynamics expounded by Freud than of ancient Roman theories of paternal absolutism *(pater potestas)*. These factors set up the affinity between Trinity and organic models of marriage, though still reflecting the hierarchical principle.

The Trinitarian theory of communion is distinctly different from strict hierarchical models, even though it maintains the patriarchal pattern of authority. It organizes itself through the interpenetration of emotional bonds arising out of the natures of the parties— natures that are to be shaped by the stewardship of the *patrimonium* received from the father. Yet this model of communion also differs markedly from the one that works out the egalitarian thrust of this symbol. The egalitarian meaning of communion finds full flower in circumstances that make possible the equal exercise of power by women and men. It is characteristic of pluralistic societies or communes.

It is easy to see how the emotional bonding of the hierarchical Trinity leads to a more organic model of family, as in the formulation "community of life and love" in *Gaudium et Spes*. Here communion is understood as community. The communion is still a familial communion, though the earlier priority of family over couple has been attenuated.

The next step beyond organic communion is found in the approach of Cornelius van der Poel, for whom there is a kind of harmonization between the interpersonal communion of the couple and the public communion of the church community and its bond with the couple. Here we still see a kind of public form of communion manifested in church, family, and couple. The emotional bond is not restricted to the couple but demands augmentation or authorization by the church. The communion of the couple, however, has become central and primary.

With Jon Nilson and Evelyn and James Whitehead, working out of a Catholic framework, and James Nelson from a Protestant one, we find the full egalitarian expression of communion. Nilson focuses on the ecstatic bond at the heart of love. The love communion at the center of God and God's creation also explodes in the communion of two lovers who become bonded in marriage. Their love is the clearest manifestation of God's love. Their marriage, though not marriage as an institution, is a symbol of the divine love.

The Whiteheads also focus on the mutual joy of shared life in communion, but then move on to stress the way marriage is a pilgrimage of personal growth. It is a more individualistic conception than Nilson's. In emphasizing the importance of equality of power in making communion possible, they are then led to accentuate the way each person can exercise his or her powers in this unique relationship.

James Nelson emphasizes both the persons expressing their power in shared life and their communion itself. He draws on aspects of covenantal thought to give structure to the way this exercise of power in the marital relationship can be kept congruent with the communion of their one flesh. Here is a sense of bodily union that verges toward the sacramental view of marriage we found in Schillebeeckx's theory of encounter.

As we have seen, communion is not automatically tied to egalitarian models of marriage. It demands not only the sociological condition of equality but also the religious inclination to ground marital life in a mystical or ecstatic approach to faith. Psychologically, it presupposes an orientation toward growth and fulfillment, rather than control or functionality. Thus it demands particular soil for its full flowering—soil widespread in contemporary culture.

Each of these symbols has its own religious base as well as various models it can appropriate. Each symbolic model makes a distinctive impact on the way we approach marriage. Each cultivates distinctive psychological orientations and demands particular ministerial responses. Each makes a contribution to a comprehensive Christian understanding of marriage and family.

In order to draw on these rich resources in our own circumstances, we need to winnow this harvest of symbolic models to find the guiding values to be sustained in marriage and family today.

Only by identifying these undergirding purposes can we develop patterns consonant with our present humanity and our religious heritage.

NOTES

1. Edward Schillebeeckx, *Marriage: Human Reality and Saving Mystery* (New York and London: Sheed & Ward, 1965), draws on the history of biblical covenant as well as sacramental theology to set forth a more interpersonal understanding of marriage as sacrament. For his theory of sacrament as redemptive encounter, see *Christ, The Sacrament of the Encounter with God* (New York and London: Sheed & Ward, 1963). For a succinct statement of Karl Rahner's approach read his "Marriage as Sacrament," in *Theological Investigations,* trans. D. Bourke (New York: Herder & Herder, 1973) 10:199–221. A more recent effort in a comparative vein is Tibor Horvath, "Marriage: Contract? Covenant? Community? Sacrament of Sacraments?—Fallible Symbol of Infallible Love, Revelation of Sin and Love," in *The Sacraments: God's Love and Mercy Actualized,* ed. F. A. Eigo (Villanova, Pa.: Villanova University Press, 1979), 143–81. For the latest pontifical formulation, see Pope John Paul II, *On the Family (Familiaris Consortio)* (Washington, D.C.: U.S. Catholic Conference, 1982).

The various interpretations of the concept of sacrament bedevil any discussion of its meaning for marriage. In accord with Rahner and Schillebeeckx, for instance, much contemporary Roman Catholic theology interprets sacrament using the concepts I have attached to the symbol of communion. This interpersonal approach to sacrament is a reaction against its earlier excessive identification with a particular institutional form that these authors now find unacceptable. My own institutional emphasis in a definition of sacrament assumes a variety of possible structures for it to legitimate. See chap. 6 n. 12.

2. For the twisting history of vocation, see Karl Holl, "Die Geschichte des Worts Beruf," *Gesammelte Aufsätze zur Kirchengeschichte, Bd. III* (Darmstadt: Wissenschaftliche Buchgesellschaft, 1965), 189–219; Alfons Auer, *Christsein im Beruf: Grundsatzliches und Geschichtliches zum christlichen Berufsethos* (Dusseldorf: Patmos-Verlag, 1966); and the classic study by Max Weber, *The Protestant Ethic and the Spirit of Capitalism,* trans. Talcott Parsons (New York: Charles Scribner's Sons, 1958).

In addition to Achtemeier's work already cited, see Stanley Hauerwas, "Sex in Public: Toward a Christian Ethic of Sex," in *A Community of Character: Toward a Constructive Christian Social Ethic* (Notre Dame, Ind.: University of Notre Dame Press, 1981), 175–95, for the heroic ethic. Søren Kierkegaard's search for a reconciliation of passion, duty, and God's command in a Christian understanding of marriage runs all through his writings, especially *Either/Or.* John Gates traces this theme through his writings in *The Life and Thought of Kierkegaard for Every-man* (Philadelphia: Westminster Press, 1960), esp. 37–90.

Barth's position appears in *Church Dogmatics* III/4; trans. A. T. McKay et al. (Edinburgh: T. & T. Clark, 1961), 170–229. For Stephen B. Clark, see chap. 3 n. 2.

For the use of vocation at Vatican II, see *Gaudium et Spes*, chaps. 47–48, 52; and for a Roman Catholic perspective, H. V. Sattler, "Marriage: Theology of," in *New Catholic Encyclopedia* (New York: McGraw-Hill, 1967) 9:265–67.

Herbert Richardson provides an opening to Rev. Sun Myung Moon's theology in "A Brief Outline of Unification Theology," in *A Time for Consideration: A Scholarly Appraisal of the Unification Church*, ed. M. Darroll Bryant and H. W. Richardson (Lewiston, N.Y.: Edwin Mellen Press, 1978), 133–40. For the Unification approach to marriage, see Young Oon Kim, *Unification Theology and Christian Thought* (New York: Unification Church, 1980), 75–80. For a sociological view, see David G. Bromley, Anson D. Shupe, and Donna L. Oliver, "Perfect Families: Visions of the Future in a New Religious Movement," in *Cults and the Family*, ed. Florence Kaslow and Marvin B. Sussman (New York: Haworth Press, 1982), 119–29.

David and Vera Mace explore marriage as a vocation in potential conflict with ministry in *What's Happening to Clergy Marriages?* (Nashville: Abingdon Press, 1980), chap. 9.

3. Since George Mendenhall pointed out the nature of covenant as a suzerainty treaty in "Law and Covenant in Israel and the Ancient Near East," *The Biblical Archaeologist* 17.2 (May 1954):26–46, and 17.3 (September 1954):49–76, others have shown other forms, some of a more egalitarian nature. For contemporary discussion of covenant, see Dennis J. McCarthy, *Old Testament Covenant: A Survey of Current Opinions* (Richmond: John Knox Press, 1972).

The shift from hierarchical patriarchy to an egalitarian, contractual form of social relationship was already set forth in Henry Maine, *Ancient Law* (Boston: Beacon Press, [1861] 1963), chap. 5. Because Roman canon law adopted contractual forms to make sacramental reality public, efforts to reform Roman Catholic approaches have tried to replace contract with its biblical relative, covenant. See Paul Palmer, "Christian Marriage: Contract or Covenant?" *Theological Studies* 33.4 (December 1972):617–65, and Tibor Horvath (see n. 1 above). Perhaps the best discussion, though still heavily psychologized, is by Jack Dominian, *Marriage, Faith and Love* (New York: Crossroad, 1982).

4. Marriage as covenant gained prominence among the Puritans and Baptists, both because of their biblicism and also because of the radical congregational experience of covenanting among equal believers to form local churches. Covenantal ideas are central to John Milton's conception of companionate marriage and his defense of divorce in "The Doctrine

and Discipline of Divorce" [1643].

The views of Adams and other Puritan thinkers can be found in *Puritan Sermons*, 1659–89 (Wheaton, Ill.: Richard O. Roberts, Pubs., 1981) 3: 548. See also the sermons in vol. 2 by Richard Steele, "What Are the Duties of Husbands and Wives Toward Each Other?" 272–302, and Richard Adams, "What are the Duties of Parents and Children; and How Are They to Be Managed According to Scripture?" 303–57. Edmund Leites (see chap. 1 n. 9) details Puritan exhortations to love one's spouse within the covenantal bond.

Wilson Yates's position is stated in "The Future of the Family, II," *Theological Markings* (United Theological Seminary of the Twin Cities), (winter 1975):16–28.

Helmut Thielicke used the concept of "the covenant of agape" in *The Ethics of Sex*, trans. J. W. Doberstein (New York: Harper & Row, 1974), 79–144.

Leonard J. Arrington and Davis Bitton place Mormon approaches to marriage and family in a historical context in *The Mormon Experience: A History of the Latter-Day Saints* (New York: Alfred A. Knopf, 1979), 185–205. See Thomas F. O'Dea, *The Mormons* (Chicago and London: University of Chicago Press, 1957), 132–43, 245–50, for a more sociological approach.

Covenant lies just beneath the surface of contemporary contractual models of marriage and family, as in John Scanzoni, *Love and Negotiate* (Waco, Tex.: Word, 1979); Earl H. Gaulke, *You Can Have a Family Where Everybody Wins: Christian Perspectives on Parent Effectiveness Training* (St. Louis: Concordia, 1975), where it is shaped by Lutheran ideas of "law and gospel"; and Sterling Honea, *Love, Sex, Marriage and Divorce* (Los Angeles: California Lawyer's Press, 1980).

5. For Bernard Häring, see chap. 3 n. 2.

Cornelius van der Poel is probably the best-known proponent of a communion model, though he is not clear about the relation of communion to community. See "Marriage and Family as Expressions of 'Communio' in the Church," *Jurist* 36.2 (1976):59–88.

Jon Nilson's stimulating position is set forth in "The Love at the Center of Love: A Theological Interpretation of Marriage," *Chicago Studies* 18.3 (fall 1979):239–50.

Evelyn and James Whitehead focus on themes of intimacy and identity dominant in communion approaches in their work, heavily influenced by Erikson's psychology, *Marrying Well: Possibilities in Christian Marriage Today* (New York: Doubleday & Co., 1981). Their own organizing symbol, however, is that of the journey.

James Nelson sees marriage as a covenant for the purpose of communion, *Embodiment: An Approach to Sexuality and Christian Theology* (Minneapolis: Augsburg, 1978), esp. 150–51.

5

Winnowing
the Harvest

THE SOCIAL EXPERIENCE

The Transitions

The subjects of marriage have not only become differentiated but the life of the persons and couple has come to the forefront of attention. This does not mean the eclipse of household and family concerns. It means that they are not the primary focus of marriage. They may flow from marriage but they do not constitute its reason for being. *← he thinks*

Moreover, it is clear that egalitarian models have surpassed their hierarchical and organic comrades in our preferences. Again, this does not mean the others are irrelevant. They simply stand in a subordinate position to a model of equality and mutuality.

In citing these transitions we must always keep in mind that they have had a certain appropriateness for different socioeconomic settings. The hierarchical household suited the survival needs of isolated agrarian human communities. Organic models served a slightly more complex form of agricultural, entrepreneurial, and artisan families. The egalitarian model arises in advanced industrial and high-technology societies. Whether we are dealing with other people pastorally, therapeutically, or politically we must remember the variety of familial worlds they may inhabit. *depends on type of culture*

People's marital and familial experiences span a vast range.

What we need to do at this point is identify the emotional and relational substance underlying these forms. What is the bond that constitutes their marriage? What is the live nerve holding these actors together? A sensitivity to these patterns of bonding can help clarify what churches are doing when they "bless the bond" of marriage. It will help us identify the lived reality people are actually experiencing so we can relate it more effectively to the symbols and values we are advancing in religion as well as in society.

The Bonds of Marriage and Family

A marriage or family endures because of a pattern of emotional bonds. These bonds are formed by the way we invest our emotions in one or another subjects of the marriage and by the model of relationship along which our emotions flow. They are matters of emotional *investment* and emotional *relationship*.

Each subject can be the focus of our emotional investment. Each can be the object of our heart's devotion. Our life may be energized by our loyalty to our children, our homemaking, our spouse, or to our own ideals—whether they be career or community standing. Marriages and families are glued together in different ways depending on where their members' emotions have been invested.[1]

In householding marriages people are bonded to the property, routines, and pattern of consumption that make up a household. They are wed to their *patrimonium*. In feudal realms this *patrimonium* may have comprised a major segment of the society. In our time the flock may have become a cat or dog, the manor an apartment, and the royal archives a scrapbook, but they have no less significance for us. In divorces, the most painful break may occur over the destruction of this household and the division of property it entails. The marriage was in fact held together by the emotional bonds of the household.

Loyalty to the household is easily transfered to the heirs who can receive, maintain, and perpetuate it after our death. The bond of parents with children can be the central bond of marriage. When "family" constitutes the emotional bond, parents are drawn in, whether consciously or not, to repeating once again the interactions they remember from their youth. We invest ourselves in marriage because it offers us a way of redoing—whether in imitation or rejection—the infantile life undergirding our basic sense of self.

Fathers often become emotionally tied to their sons—their heirs, whether in personality or property. Mothers may love their daughters as companions and their sons as future protectors. By extension these emotional bonds link them outward to uncles, aunts, grandparents, and cousins. It is the family itself that is the frame of their emotional bonds.

When the emotional bond lies between the spouses, their common enterprise is no longer primarily a household or a family. It is their life together, whether in leisure, community activities, or work. They no longer act as members of a family of origin or simply as parents, but as a couple. They are held together by the resonance arising out of the similarities of their personalities, even though nurtured by unique backgrounds and experiences. Here, the injunction of Genesis "to leave your mother and father and become one flesh" takes on an emotional rather than a patrimonial meaning.

We can even speak about the emotional bond of a marriage focused on persons. Here the marriage and family is subordinate to the aims of each person. The husband/father may be invested in his career and need a household for necessities and a family for respectability. The wife/mother may actually be emotionally involved with religion. Her marital role is the outworkings of these loyalties. This is a centripetal situation, since the marriage or family itself is emotionally barren. It has been a widespread phenomenon, however, often fostered by the social or religious idealization of family life.

The reason we have lifted up these patterns of bonding is that they are the source of energy by which people sustain themselves as children, spouses, and parents. The bond of marriage is no one thing. In trying to bless it we need to know what we are blessing. In attempting to heal it we need to know what we are healing. In consoling its destruction we must know what is breaking.

The pattern of bonding is the motor that enables us to pursue the values we attach to marriage. It is this emotional structure that determines what people can and cannot do in marriage. This is the emotional ground on which we must set forth the values framing our religious response to marriage in our own time.

THE GUIDING VALUES

Emotional bonds create energy and articulate forms for living. They shape our aspirations and desires. Now we must identify the values that can guide our actions in marriage and family. What values are in evidence within the vast harvest of symbolic models lived out in our history? To answer this question we shall begin with the motives at work in our emotional bonds. We must clarify the ways people are bound into the varied relationships of domestic life. We see that the varying models manifest distinctive personal goods which can be realized in them. They can shape our character in certain ways and give us certain enjoyments and blessings. These may not be the social or ecclesial purposes of marriage, but we prize these fruits for their significance to us as persons.

We can then consider the enduring societal and ecclesial purposes pursued in marriage and family. In lifting up the purposes of marriage we also establish grounds for its formal dissolution. Sometimes these grounds arise from the church's purposes. The marriage fails as a reality of faith or grace. It fails, from an institutional standpoint, to advance the church's purposes. Other times it fails as a matter of creation. It fails to achieve the purposes set forth by social institutions. Divorce has always been recognized. It is only the grounds that have shifted. The grounds exist already in the purposes. Clarifying these purposes will also help us understand the grounds for divorce.[2] Examining changing grounds for divorce helps us clarify in turn the purposes of marriage and family.

In this search for enduring values we will be looking for key themes to be honored in developing a contemporary theological approach to marriage. We will then establish some theological principles for tying these values together in the framework of faith.

Personal Motives

The broad shift from household to person and from hierarchy to equality brings to the fore distinctive personality structures and personal values. People's motivations for entering into marriage are the complex fruit of the emotional structure energizing their lives and the values they see as indispensable for worthwhile living.

Earlier I pointed out the great difficulty in identifying the personal motives for entering marriage. Because of their private character it is even harder to generalize about them. Sometimes these motives appear as conscious reasons, which may differ from the culturally or ecclesially approved purposes for marriage. Other times they are "reasons of the heart," removed from our conscious awareness. In either case these reasons are so multitudinous and murky that it is hard to talk about this human experience. The importance of this interior dimension of our lives demands, however, that we make some account of it and press toward some theory about the values it bears.

To negotiate this difficult terrain I propose three steps. First, we need some theory for understanding the values and purposes at work in people's motives. We need to identify the values present in the psychology of the various models of marriage and family. The two general motives I will identify for this purpose are *expression* and *confirmation.*

Second, we need to see how these underlying motives have generated certain kinds of characteristic personality patterns within the framework of the various models.

Third, we shall examine three values widely associated with marriage—love, sex, and sacrifice—in order to see the impact of these epochal transitions on people's ethical aspirations. In short, in this section we will lay down the natural base, the anthropology, that must guide our constructive theological effort in the last chapter.

 Expression and Confirmation

My working hypothesis is that people have sought the values of expression and confirmation through the various models of marriage. These personal motives are deeply rooted in human psychology. They form a natural substratum on which we can erect a viable understanding of the personal values appropriate for marriage in our own time. What then are the meanings of these two terms and what kinds of experiences give rise to this supposition?

By *expression* I simply mean the drive to bring forth something that is our mark in the world. It is an effort to establish the reality of our own initiative, creativity, and uniqueness. It is a profession of self by which others might be aware of our existence.

By *confirmation* I mean the response we receive to this act of expression. What we want in this response is some kind of confirmation if not affirmation. We want to know we share a common world with some others. We have our existence not merely in expressing what is within us but in sharing a common world. Confirmation is a word summing up the good we seek in sensing some stable framework of reality by which we can make our way in life.

These two personal motives can be pursued in various ways. We can express ourselves in many ways, just as there are many social worlds that can confirm our lives. These motives both energize us and guide us. They are drives as well as values. The various marital models are modes of expression and confirmation. They are ways that people have tried to pursue these fundamental human values. How then are these motives manifested in the various models?

Motives and Models

Hierarchical models revolve around relationships of command and control. Not only is the superior seeking to control the inferiors, but the inferiors seek to control themselves as well as to control the superior by various devious means.

The relationship of command and control reinforces a bond of dependency and service. The superior needs the services of the inferior. The inferior depends on the protection and direction of the superior. As Richard Sennett points out, authority must nurture even as the dependent must obey. Hierarchy is a particular form of reciprocity creating a deep bond.[3]

Psychologically this is a bond of fear, rage, and resentment alternating with gratitude and devotion. It is unstable because the actors can always threaten to overturn the delicate imbalance between their statuses. The superior can use the power of nurture to thwart the needs of the inferior. The inferior can withhold services in an incipient rebellion fueled by rage and fear. It is in the interest of the superior that this rage be turned against the inferior in guilty self-abnegation. It is in the interest of the inferior that the superior's power be turned against its excess by appeal to the superior's ideology of benevolence and noblesse oblige.

People in hierarchies are preoccupied with questions of *status.*

How does one stand in the relation of superior and subordinate? Actions are geared to confirmation of this hierarchy. Anger and resentment over departure from status mingle with dispositions to care and service. Shame is the dominant motivating force in maintaining correct standing before the others.

In this context how we appear to others is crucial. Deception becomes necessary to maintain standing. It becomes a natural way of life as we seek to prevent impulses toward expression of equality or performance from interfering with the hierarchical icon of status. What must be safeguarded above all is honor, whether this is manifested in virginity, potency, or manners.

To survive in such situations women have had to resort to stratagems that men have then labeled "devious." This is frequently the psychological struggle going on between parents and children as well as husbands and wives. Hierarchy demands that conflicts be resolved by appeal to the status prerogatives of superiors, rather than common goals or a compromise of interests.

The tables indicated that hierarchical models tend toward the family and household subjects, because this is where hierarchical relations can be spelled out most fully and where command and control are most necessary for survival. The need for command hierarchies grows in proportion to the number of members and activities regulated by the marriage. Moreover, the intrinsic inequality between parents and children finds a natural basis in hierarchical relations. There is a natural affinity between hierarchy and household.

Though their members often change, families and households are arenas of expression and confirmation. Households are both expressions of ourselves in tangible things and also confirmations of us with their enduring familiarity—furniture, artifacts, utensils, and mementos. People express themselves even more vitally through their children and try to get confirmation from them. Children are an earthly memory as well as intimate respondents to the spontaneous dramatics of our life. Moreover, when the children become adults, they in turn can replicate the patterns of their childhood in a new family.

In this pattern of replication we seek to preserve the most confirming emotional experiences of our lives—our infantile relations with our parents. In relations of parental subordination we find comfort and confirmation. It is as a parent that we seek to express ourselves in adult life. These relations, of course, are necessarily hierarchical. Our emotional disposition in the family therefore tends by necessity toward hierarchy.

In both the household and family we find a pattern of confirmation that is inherently bound up with control—whether over things or over children. They are both kinds of property by which we express ourselves. Their confirmation of us usually has to happen within the ambit of our control over them. Because of this control factor, the confirming world created by the parent gains in certitude what it loses in comprehensiveness. The parent can be confirmed and affirmed by a fairly controlled world, but this confirmation does not enable him or her to go very far beyond the household.

This motive of control has a further psychological side. The familial household required the sacrifice of personal expression to the need for external confirmation and survival. Emotional expression, far from fueling the marriage, threatened to destroy its hierarchical structure. Life in marriage was a denial of feelings, a constant state of incongruity between feeling, thought, and action. The self was best typified as a cauldron in conflict—the classic Freudian model.

These patterns have constituted the daily emotional life of hierarchical marriages for centuries. They are the raw experience underlying much of our religious and cultural life. They are the psychological side of the values of obedience, sacrifice, and altruistic benevolence. They are rooted in the natural inequalities of parenthood and property control. While we may no longer wish to shape marriage in their image, we must take account of their dynamics in domestic life.

Organic relationships revolve not around the reciprocity between one status and the other but in the relation of each member to the common good. They are concerned more with role and function than status and control. Organic models rest on functionality. Each member occupies a role ordered to the functioning of the whole. Here we count not so much on the other members for our reward and confirmation as on the success of the common task, whether it be children, business, or religious service. Here obedience to persons in a higher status (child to parent, wife to husband) is offset by functional importance to system survival.

The emotional dynamics of this model are not carried on directly between two persons but between the self and the bearer of the goal. It may be the family, the church, community, or nation. In any case our motives are characterized by aspiration and failure, self-esteem and guilt. We are, however, not so much concerned about status—as in the hierarchical model—as with achievement, productivity, and functionality. We are invested more in our work and activity than in our immediate standing before superiors. We are concerned more for what we have done than for who we are.

In this model the strength of our bonds rests more on the success of the whole against its environment than on the actions of one of the members toward another. It is the success of the marital system itself that counts. The organic model thus creates a bond of common tasks on whose success the survival of the whole depends. It develops an ethos of complementarity when applied to couples and an ethos of functional differentiation in its family and household forms. Mother, father, and children all have their tasks and roles, whether to secure income, prepare the meals, or carry out the garbage.

In organic models people are concerned with *role performance* and *cooperation*. Achievement and production become central values as each seeks to make a proper contribution to the good of the whole. This is not an individualistic aspiration but an effort to act as a cooperative member of the group. Here we might find the guilt and remorse of failure but not the rage and resentment of unequal status. We experience guilt as we measure ourselves against some objective value that we have internalized. In hierarchies, on the other hand, we experience shame as we measure ourselves against the status prerogatives of other persons.

Here the virtues of industry, productivity, and cooperation replace those of honor. The mute testimony of our deeds replaces the appearance of standing. Cooperation supplants obedience in service to the whole. The system is the unseen god that measures our lives regardless of the superficial opinions of others. In its classic form we become obligated to "do it for the sake of the family" above all else.

Egalitarian bonds involve direct reciprocity between actors equal in power. They are related neither by hierarchical command nor by their roles in a system. Their emotional bond rests in the dense combination of agreements made possible by their personal similarity. While the organic model can accept a wide variety of personalities, each making his or her own contribution to the whole, the egalitarian model assumes similarity of personality in order to provide the common base on which to negotiate all the distinct issues that may arise in a rapidly changing situation.

Here control gives way to negotiation, and negotiation to discernment of resonant nodes of cooperation. The psychology necessary for this demands congruence of feeling and thought. It demands personal responsibility for action rather than a resort to scapegoating. It constrains us to confront present issues rather than claim that overpowering divine or demonic forces are causing female hysteria and male domination. It demands honest communication. Survival of the marriage depends on personal expression rather than repression.

In this context our expression occurs through our own communication rather than through children or household property. We express the creations of our imagination in words, gestures, symbols. To develop the inner world of consciousness we seek personal development, expression, and companionship. We become performers to our partner. Loneliness is feared even more than starvation. Friendship is desired above public position. Lack of friendship in marriage, rather than being an assumption, becomes an exquisite torture whose only relief is divorce.

In this communicative world of mutual expression the partners themselves constitute the confirming world created by their marriage. Because of the premium communication places on mutual understanding, it presses us toward an equality of the persons in marriage. Each must be able to resonate with the emotional and mental frame of the other in order to confirm and be confirmed in their interaction.

This process of confirmation can be very intense and affirming, but also very fragile and precarious. It gains in intensity what it loses in stability. While the immediate world it creates is quite small, it can introduce the persons to quite complex larger worlds based on communication. Indeed, unless the confirmation of this conjugal world is strong, they are thrust into much wider public worlds to find arenas of expression and confirmation. There is no buffering household to absorb these needs. The partners enter immediately into more impersonal publics from the intimacy of their communion.

In egalitarian relationships we are moved by concern for *identity*. The power dynamics among the persons rest on intensification or removal of confirming affection. Fear of losing the words and presence of the partner alternates with the desire to be united with the mate. Therefore intimacy becomes paramount because we need the immediate resonance with the other to confirm our inner existence. This demands full disclosure from the partner. Honesty, openness, and sharing stand at the opposite extreme from the concern for appearance and the deviousness typical of hierarchical models. Mutuality replaces reciprocity or obedience in people's expectations. We seek to mirror each other rather than imitate an objective hierarchical chain of being or a cosmos of functions. We seek to express who we really are, even when it interrupts the efficient functioning of the relationship or calls into question the self-understanding of the other person.

This model is most appropriate where family and household are subordinate concerns. It has a natural affinity for marriage focused on persons and couples. As life spans lengthen it becomes the natural model for marriage. It does not attend to the inequalities between parents and children. It is not ordered to efficient functioning as much as to the intrinsic reward of mutuality. The marriage revolves around the needs of the persons rather than the demands of the organic whole.

From the standpoint of the organicists it is functionless. From the viewpoint of hierarchicalists it is prone to permissive hedonism. Regardless of our moral evaluations, this model fits a world where survival needs are pursued by extrafamilial institutions, where the life of the couple outlasts their family-household, and power is shared by men and women.

Motives and models have a complex interrelationship. We can summarize our discussion so far in this way. This transition from hierarchical and organic models of family and household to egalitarian models for couples brings with it a train of value changes. Our personal values are shaped by our choice of marital subject

and marital model. Each model is held together by a different pattern of emotional investment and relationship: that of inequality,
of complementarity, and of similarity. The conditions of adequate
bonding differ markedly in the three models just as their dominant
values do.

In the hierarchical model usually associated with family and
household we seek the values of *parenthood* and parental status.
We seek renewal of the population, socialization of the young, and
defense against external dangers. Dependency constitutes its fundamental experience.

In organic models we espouse *cooperative membership* for the
sake of the family system. People are equal as members of the
whole, even though they may exercise different functions and powers and occupy different statuses. What counts is participation in
the common enterprise for which each is indispensable.

When we enter the world of the egalitarian couple we embrace
the values of identity through *friendship.* The resonant mutuality,
intercourse, and reciprocal confirmation between equals identify
them as unique selves and create a world of mutual confirmation
between them. Their identity is worked out in their relationship as
equals in power.

Each of these are valued patterns of relationship. Each yields a
peculiar preoccupation that shapes our lives and gives them their
meaning. The three models bear characteristic implications for
personality.[4] They cultivate certain typical dispositions, expectations, and dynamics. They are differing means for achieving expression and confirmation in our lives. They are ways we clothe the
motives of our heart with values for the public world.

To the outsider these differences may seem minor, but to those
who have experienced them, they are enormous. The same energy
that mobilizes these relationships can also destroy them. Two people operating out of different models can find themselves in a
dance of death. In order to feel the bite of these changes more specifically let us examine their significance for the values of love, sex,
and sacrifice.

Love, Sex, and Sacrifice

Love, sex, and sacrifice do not have univocal meanings, as many
of us find out to our consternation. The shift from hierarchy to

equality, from sacrificial obedience to creative expression, and from patriarchy to mutuality deeply affects their meaning and the values they bear.

In a hierarchical framework love means paternal care. It is the continual reaffirmation of a world that gives security to the loved one. It is a love emphasizing a stable world of confirmation in which we find expression through procreation and property. It is the love of parent for child, now transferred to the maternal love of the wife for the husband as son and the paternal love of the husband for the wife as daughter.

Moreover, sexual relations are oriented toward children and the maintenance of stable property relations. For women in patriarchal society—the classic form of hierarchical householding—sex meant the confirmation of dependence, whether in being restricted to the household, dying in childbirth, or submitting to male prerogative. It is amazing that any women could celebrate sex at all in that situation. For the male, of course, sex was the means for maintaining *patrimonium,* property, and worldly status through procreation, as well as for obtaining relatively safe physical gratification. Little wonder that males have extolled it so. We cannot here probe all the complexities of these psychodynamics, which are intense, profound, and elaborate. We can only note the dominant form in which they have occurred.

In the organic model love is the care for the whole. Emotional energy is fastened to the family or household as such. We express ourselves in the fulfillment of our role and we are confirmed in accord with that role performance. Love is care for the system as such.

Similarly, sexual relations are a means of confirming one's membership in the system of relations, not as superior and subordinate but as members with an obligation to the welfare of the whole. That is, women have children in order to satisfy the needs of the family rather than of the husband. Sexuality is a means for enhancing the man's self-esteem in order to perform his role better, rather than to confirm his status alone. Sexuality moves from being a symbol of domination to one of membership in an overarching whole. The exploitation of patriarchy is tempered with the obligations of role performance.

In egalitarian love we find emotional attachment to the other as friend. Both initiate, both respond. The persons are loved as brother and sister rather than as parent and child. The emotional paradigm is rooted in sibship rather than parenthood. Partnership replaces subordination or membership in the whole.

Likewise, sexual relations are symbols of mutual freedom, intimate affirmation, and friendly intercourse. They are modeled on childlike play rather than parental care or ritual performance. They exist for their own sake as a mode of intense bodily communication rather than as a means for children or security.

Many people would immediately call this a "selfish" approach to marriage. The marriage revolves around the selves. In a technical sense, it *is* "self-ish." Several qualifications are in order, however. First, every marriage, to the extent it serves the interests or needs of the selves involved, has a selfish dynamic. This is often masked over, as in the patriarchal models, so that even the service of the man's interests appears as a sacrificial obligation of running a household for the sake of the community.

Second, we see the ways that spiritual commitments of the persons also constitute their marital selfishness. The altruistic loyalties that serve communal and religious interests can also function very selfishly in the marriage. The fact that there can be personal models of marriage in a religious framework underscores this ambiguity. The accusation of selfishness arises in the conflict between models of marriage anchored in different subjects. Persons are seen as selfishly expressing their identity over preserving their coupling. Couples are seen as selfishly ignoring the family. Families selfishly pursue their mobile, nuclear existence oblivious to the virtues of stable households. Selfishness, then, like so many other values, has to be seen in the context of wider religious, psychological, and societal meanings.

Love does indeed entail a willingness to sacrifice for the beloved, but in the shift to person and couple, sacrifice, though still recognized as a value, is limited by its purpose. Not any and every sacrifice is justified by the marital structure. Personal integrity, creativity, and development of one's powers are not themselves to be sacrificed but are the reasons why people would sacrifice other values. In short, the ends of sacrifice receive new content and meaning.

Moreover, we can see the ways old theories of sacrifice were also highly ideological. They masked exploitation as much as they evoked loyalty. To say, for instance, that Christ's sacrifice for the church was symbolized in the father's relationship to the wife and children obscured the fact that it was the wife who did all the sacrificing—her name, her public potentials, her will, and person. The same dynamic functioned in vocational symbols which emphasized obedience, in covenantal formulations stressing suzerainty, and in communion symbols of male precedence. Awareness of the distinctive integrity and claims of persons and their friendship as a couple challenges automatic analogies between religious symbols and marriage that obscure these egalitarian values.

These distinct meanings of love cannot be fitted easily into the traditional distinctions of *agape, philia,* and *eros.*[5] It is worth noting, however, that agape is clearly related to the parental love of the hierarchical family and household. *Philia* and eros both find residence in the egalitarian relationship. I am, however, holding that all the forms are "erotic" in the sense of being patterns of intense emotional attachment. What is important here is the emotional structuring of our dispositions, rather than the traditional moralistic focus on the spectrum between selfishness (eros) and altruism (agape).

Love's meaning, then, is embedded in the network of trust by which we launch ourselves into a world of dependable expectations. It is the ship in which the engines of expression and confirmation can move us to our destinies. These questions of love, sex, and sacrifice press us to wider social and religious values. They lead us ultimately to the foundations of trust known in faith. Let us first see the implications of this transition in values for social and ecclesial arenas before pressing on to these theological grounds.

Societal Purposes

Societal purposes for marriage are summed up in *children* and *security.* These are the two main values that societies have sought to achieve through the various institutions of marriage. Societies historically have needed children in order to replenish their productive powers. They have needed to provide for people's security in order to maintain a stable order.

Children are foremost when societies are labor-intensive or where infant mortality is high. This has been the case in almost all previous societies, with scattered exceptions among the upper classes in the ancient Mediterranean. Children may be needed not only for productive work. They may also be needed for warfare. Where the factors of warfare, labor-intensive production, and high infant mortality decline, societal need for children declines as well. In our own time we find a widespread withdrawal, especially in China, India, and the industrialized world, from valuing reproduction and supporting marriages that achieve it. Of course, China and India pursue reduced reproduction in order to curb consumption of food. Industrialized countries do so to allocate more resources to education of a highly skilled labor force.

Curtailment of reproduction need not be confined to policies regarding married people. Where marriage is still to be oriented to reproduction societies may restrict permission to marry until couples can establish a household. This is usually carried out by legitimating the parents' right to withhold property from their children until they approve of a proposed marriage. This was a widespread practice in Europe, surviving in Ireland almost to the present day.

When concern for education overrides reproduction, we see the classic context for vocational models. Whereas reproductive societies punished contraception and rewarded reproduction, these societies reward and assist the educational efforts of families. Indeed, they are positively intrusive in their demand that children have an education outside the home and that parents treat their children as citizens of the society with rights and liberties of their own.

The grounds for divorce in child-focused societies turn on the parents' capacity to produce and socialize children. This may take a number of forms. In patriarchal societies the woman's inability to conceive is grounds for divorce. The church tried to curtail this ground, a struggle culminating in the split between Rome and Henry VIII, who demanded a son of his wives to stabilize the throne's succession. To underscore its opposition to divorce on such grounds the church also emphasized that childless couples could build up the church in their own way.[6] Societally, however, the lack of widespread divorce on these grounds was probably due

to the social need to provide for the security of daughters una$\,$
return to their family.

In societies emphasizing the education of children we see the
rise of the state's ability to divorce children from parents who are
not raising them to be productive citizens.[7] This is a familial rather
than a couple divorce, occasioned by the parents' inability to care
for the child, who is above all a citizen of the state. In these situations, the state's concern for children takes priority over its concern for the parents and their parental rights or even their bond,
which may be grounded, no matter how twistedly, in the children
they abuse. Regardless of our evaluation of the ethical outcome of
this development, it manifests a deep distinction in our own time
between conjugal, parental, and child rights. Its implications are
profound for both society and the church.

Societal concern for security takes a number of forms, embracing property transfer, legitimation of authority, and economic welfare as well as pyschological well-being. We must note, however,
that it is the society that has the right to security. This societal
demand was first registered against the household. Households
must be maintained in order that general social order can be
secured. This was a frequent goal of the Hebrew prophets as well
as a major concern of the Roman republic. Only more recently
have we seen a social interest in advancing the rights of couples
and persons as a means for social security.

Where marriage is the means for establishing and managing
productive households, the society seeks to maintain marriages in
order to handle the orderly transfer of property, the transfer of
control over land, and—with monarchical and feudal orders—the
transfer of governmental power itself. Prohibitions against divorce
must be seen as efforts to maintain social order under these conditions.

Prohibitions against adultery have had a similar impact. Here,
however, under the conditions of biology and patriarchy they were
to guarantee legitimacy of heirs. In its primal form the prohibition
of adultery and its use as the sole basis for divorce was an appeal to
male right. It was females who could not be adulterous or whose
adultery was actually punished, for their adultery would call into

question the ancestry of their children, their claim to legitimacy, and thereby the exercise of their rights as holders of social power and duties. The structure of monarchy and feudal order depended on clear legitimacy. Even to this day, the meaning of adultery is quite different in family-household marriages than in those focusing on the couple.

These sanctions against adultery did not rest merely on the biological fact that children can be traced more easily to their mothers than to their fathers. Male privilege with regard to adultery also rested on the need to preserve the structure of authority and dominance seen as necessary in the wider society. Marriages must create children who are socialized into patriarchal forms of legitimate authority. The fact that the woman bore the burden of prohibitions against adultery emphasized this preeminence of the father, even when biology would not.

As we move away from households as the bearers of social order and economic production we see fewer social efforts to prevent divorce. Household functions are carried on by corporations, educational institutions, and political organizations. Marriage need not be responsible for these functions. Similarly, as patriarchy yields to a rational order based on personal technological achievement, divorce based on adultery loses its legal if not psychological centrality.

This is not at all to say, however, that the major institutions lose all interest in sustaining marriages, whether by prohibiting divorce or by other means. Wherever the social order depends on the capacity of individuals to interact stably in complex and changing situations, it has an interest in cultivating those kinds of personalities. The major way it does so is by enhancing the intimate sphere in which persons gain the subtle yet powerful reinforcements of prestige, self-esteem, creative power, and courage to face public life. In these situations a great deal of social energy goes into providing supports and social services for the achievement of these marital goals. Similarly, society does not try to hold two people together who destroy each other's self-esteem and psychological health. Society limits itself to a concern for the honoring of property contracts and social justice, as in the equitable division of spousal property and the raising of children. This is the major direction of family law in the high-technology countries.[8]

These then are the basic purposes of marriage as they are manifested in a number of forms and social conditions. It is clear that the pursuit of these enduring social purposes—children and security—need not always be attached to marriage itself. There are a variety of ways for achieving these ends, both within and without marriage. These forms may or may not be compatible with church purposes, though over time there is great pressure for convergence.

In both cases, from the standpoint of the church as well as of society, the purposes set up grounds for publicly recognized divorce. Just as marriage or the family is no one thing socially, so neither is divorce or the grounds for allowing it. These facts we need to keep in mind as we press toward an appropriate theological understanding of marriage in our own time.

From a theological standpoint the wider societal purposes of marriage arise from its standing as a part of nature, as part of God's creation. While they can be grounded theologically these purposes are distinct from those flowing directly from the church. Ecclesial values, on the other hand, flow first of all from the understanding of marriage as a reality of grace. They are expressions of the redemptive processes of God. Let us now examine them in a search for the enduring values that we must take account of in formulating a theology of marriage which honors both redemptive grace and the good creation.

Ecclesial Purposes

As I said at the beginning, the early church's limited interest in marriage was completely subordinated to its belief in the imminent and cataclysmic advent of God's perfect order. Its purpose, if it had one, was to minimize the importance of marriage. Once the euphoric expectation of the end had passed, however, Christians began to develop explicit purposes with regard to marriage. The church saw in marriage a means for accomplishing spiritual ends. The various symbolic models have arisen to express several different values arising from Christian faith.

Sacramental models usually focus on building up the church, the body of Christ. Households and families exist to socialize people into the faith through the regular routines of their life. They are the nursery of the church. The little church created by marriage raises up children of the faith to be children of God. Church sacraments legitimate the structure of authority that undergirds the family as a taken-for-granted world in which people can grow in a trustworthy, dependable environment. In this way marriage exists to serve the church. In doing so, of course, it also replenishes the society.

This focus on reproduction and socialization is most appropriate to a fairly settled cultural situation. At least the *form* of legitimate institutions is a settled matter, in spite of wars, natural disasters, and population movements. Thus, it was the approach characteristic of the Christendom era. Its most favorable economic context is one demanding labor—the replenishment of the population. Hence agrarian life, especially that of the family farm, occupies a prominent place. The concern for labor and family solidarity, however, can also be transferred to urban labor markets, where it takes a viable but attenuated form. There, the formerly productive woman is confined to consumption decisions in the home, and the children gradually become consumers of education rather than producers of goods. In either case, sacramental ritual, stable forms of legitimate authority, and marriage as means for socialization of workers into key institutions, including the church, fit together in a coherent combination.

Historically, these models have accepted divorce when a marriage interfered with the relation of one of the spouses to the church. Here we find the famous Pauline "privilege of the faith," in which Christians married to unbelievers could divorce them if the marriage threatened their faith. We find it also in the late medieval church's readiness to declare marriages invalid where the couple did not intend to have children. Both of these conditions threatened the ability of the marriage to build up the church and socialize new members of the society.

The primary purpose for marriage in *vocational approaches* is to serve God and the Kingdom of God. Marriages are key partners with the church in responding to God's call to give witness to the divine order. Marriage is an instrument of God's governance. Married people and families are to serve God by transforming the world. The family, as a unit, is a disciple of Christ. This is very apparent in the role played by the minister's family in Protestant churches, where this symbol is especially powerful.

Because vocational models stress the direct relation between God and the subject, they are much more characteristic of unsettled times. In the midst of social change and uncertainty, where the traditional authorities fail, vocation calls us to obedience to a transcendent God worthy of our devotion. Vocation establishes a sense of mission and destiny that overcomes the chaos of the world. Thus, it is not surprising to see its appeal rise in times of revolutionary conflict or social change.

Since vocational models stress the achievement of goals within a defined framework of meaning, they are peculiarly appropriate where there is a complex division of labor. Vocational models assume that each member of the family will have a primary call to some special work in the wider world. This at least is the more personal form, which has an affinity for a specialized economy demanding the acquisition of personal skills outside the home. Moreover, it assumes an attenuation of family ties for the sake of pursuing one's vocation wherever God calls. When only the man had a public vocation, this model produced the mobile nuclear family. Today, with both spouses exercising a public vocation, we see commuting couples operating from a household headquarters.

When the family or household itself is the subject of the call, we come closer to the family farm or cottage industry context. Even here, however, the focus is on the common work and not on the wider natural order of kinship relations. There is a distinctively different ethos that disposes the vocational family away from raising children and toward the pursuit of goals in the wider world. Thus, vocational family models fit in well with the specialized and rapidly changing world of an industrial society oriented to the pursuit of rational goals, whether these are defined by a socialist state or a capitalist market.

The earliest way a concern for vocation served as the ground for divorce was in the case of one partner entering the religious life. The religious life was the one institutional form given to vocation for many centuries. To my knowledge no other form of this ground for divorce has emerged. The modern secularized form of it arises when marriages break down because of divergent career patterns. This, however, has never been a formalized ground, either in the church or in civil society, though it is an accepted motive in some circles.

Covenantal models take this sense of mission even further. Not only is marriage an instrument of God. It is also a model of God's covenantal order. It is a new and distinct community among communities. Members relate to each other as partners in covenant and not merely as disciples of the Lord. They are not only to *build* a new world. They are to *be* a new world.

Covenantal models are also well fitted to times of social change. But here we find the creation of new communal forms at the center. In this sense they are a reaction against the isolated impersonality of a highly rational economy. They express a resurgent longing for the intimate confirmation of community. Covenants express the development of new forms of relationships. Though they result from struggle, negotiation, and willpower, they do provide new islands of stability in a sea of change. They rest on rocks of emerging consensus after the flood. Covenantal models are appropriate to times of change moving toward new consolidation.

Covenantal models, in stressing patterns of relationships, center the grounds of divorce in the breaking of these normative bonds. To the degree that covenant is identified with a contractualist approach to marriage, any violation of the marriage contract is grounds for divorce. To the degree that church membership is equated with covenant, breaking this ecclesial bond can dissolve the marriage. Many sectarian groups move in this direction, drawing on the scriptural precedent of the Pauline privilege. The reality of divorce as a result of exclusion from the ethnic faith community is far more extensive. Here the church community is so embedded in ethnic ties that violation of these bonds is practically equivalent to the breach of faith associated with ecclesial grounds for divorce.

The foremost ground for divorce on the basis of breaking covenant, however, is adultery. Here the pledge of mutual fidelity is broken. In patriarchal societies this ground can be invoked only by the male. Jesus and, in the sixth century, Justinian extended this to men and women alike. While adultery as grounds for divorce has other bases in societal purposes, it is also a peculiarly Christian one in that it bespeaks the breaking of covenant—the form of our relationship with God and all other people.

With *communion models* the church seeks to empower persons. It seeks to energize them in their marital and familial relationships so that they can accomplish their vocation, live out their covenant, and participate in the sacrament of life. It is much more accepting of people's natures. Rather than trying to transform them directly or approach them as instruments or members of a community, it tries to give them the power to reveal themselves to each other so that in the resonance between their revealed selves they might be transformed to higher levels of living. Out of their love and praise others can be evoked to greater love and lives of thankful service.

Because communion models can be seen as the energizing level beneath all the others, we can expect to find them in a subordinate role in all times, whether in Solomon's court, the medieval manor, or the Victorian parlor. It does, however, seek a particular kind of context for its fuller flowering. Wherever persons stand out as individuals the communion model finds a fitting place. Just as persons are empowered in communion, so communion requires individuals as preconditions for a marriage based on likeness of nature rather than obedience to authority, fulfillment of role, or participation in common tasks. The development of higher degrees of personal individuation may be part of social change, as when persons are liberated from confining and oppressive structures. But individuation may also be a basic way of life in a society where relationships of status and power result from personal initiative rather than communal position. We might say, somewhat imprecisely, that communion is appropriate to situations of orderly change.

Though communion models have many possible contexts, they do exhibit a political bias, whereas the others have historically been fixed on agrarian, industrial, or postindustrial life. With communion, we find models appropriate to high technology contexts, where the means of communication have been enhanced and refined to an extraordinary extent. Because of advanced communication, a greater plurality of types of people can interact, making old kinship dependencies precarious and demanding greater communication skills in establishing the bases for common life.

This emphasis on communication disposes us to political models of life—those emphasizing the capacity for speech, action, negotiation, discernment of interests and conditions for compromise. Communion marriage rests on these skills and the condition of individualization arising in a highly politicized, communicative society.

Marriages based on communion purposes dissolve when their energizing love is irretrievably dead. They only exist on the basis of mutual acceptance, equality of friendship, and the erotic bond of lovers. If those disappear the marriage is finished. The only question we may have is whether the love is retrievable. Here we explore whether the grounds for communion exist—similarity, compatibility, equality, freedom, and, above all, communicative capacity. If these are markedly lacking a marriage of communion is impossible. It should be dissolved lest people deny their personal dignity and turn a means of graceful empowerment into a destructive pretense.

Christians therefore approach marriage in distinctively different ways in each case: to build up the church, to serve God, to create a new world, and to empower persons. These are all enduring Christian purposes. The church's decision to achieve those purposes through marriage has depended on specific historical conditions and cultural contexts. That they should be pursued in general flows from the imperatives of faith. Whether they should be pursued through marriage is a question demanding reasonable response. To answer this question we need to turn to the theological bases for Christian engagement with marriage and family. First we will examine the significance of our major transitions for the key Christian symbols and then for the concept of faith itself.

THE KEY SYMBOLS
IN THEOLOGICAL PERSPECTIVE

The key marital symbols perform many functions in Christian thought and action. We have already seen how they uphold differing values concerning marriage and shape differing understandings of its purpose. They thereby mold the church's understanding of its own purposes with regard to it. Each symbol lifts up a characteristic set of virtues to be advanced in married life. Now, to move toward our constructive effort we need to see how they emphasize different assumptions about the relation of nature and grace. In so doing we can see how each symbol has its own characteristic approach to faith as it is expressed in marriage. In clarifying our understanding of nature, grace, and faith we lay the foundation for a contemporary theology of marriage and family.

Theological Foundations:
Nature and Grace

The relationship between nature and grace is theological shorthand for discussing the relation of the "what is" to the "what might be," of the existing social order to the anticipated new order in God, of the world to the church. Each of these symbols has its characteristic way of relating these two dimensions of faith life.

Sacrament emphasizes the presence of God's power in the symbolic actions of the church. But this church is not isolated from the world and from nature. It embraces them in order to redeem and lift them up. With regard to marital models, it tends to accept readily the existing models offered by the culture. With regard to subjects, however, it tends to focus on that which offers the widest entree into the total society. It does this in order to embrace the world in a comprehensive fashion. Therefore, sacramental models have tended to stress household and family, since they combined so many elements of economics, governance, education, and property control. In the process they have taken on and legitimated the patriarchal form of household and family typical of most cultures to our day.

Sacramental action takes up natural forms—in the past the existing structure of patriarchy—and "perfects" them. It "graces" nature. What this means sociologically is that it provides vivid and compelling symbolizations of these social relationships, expresses them with clarity and precision, and thereby legitimates a certain pattern of life. It provides an authoritative structure and socializes people into it so that they conscientiously behave in closer and closer conformity with the ideal.

While the sacramental approach eschews coercion and exclusionary tactics it nevertheless becomes increasingly identified with a particular social order from which it has derived its primal symbols. In the course of cultural change it can therefore take on a more absolutistic sectarian bent as it tries to preserve the old order. This has been the experience of strongly sacramental churches in our own time. While in theory they can be open to whatever cultural models exist in their society, their sacralization of earlier cultural forms makes it difficult for them to adjust to new ones.

Finally, because sacramental approaches see grace embracing the world, they tend to view marriage as a natural symbol of faith. The "is-ness" of existing marital models appears highly compatible with the "ought-ness" implied by grace. In terms of our earlier distinction between symbols *of* and metaphors *for* faith, sacrament emphasizes marriage as a symbol manifesting the claims of faith. It is lifted up as a channel of grace. Grace is the power to live up to and "live into" the natural forms of marriage. While this gives sacraments a strategic position for empowering people to fulfill their social roles, it tends to cultivate once again an overly rigid sacralization of these roles.

Vocation usually creates a tension between nature and grace. Here grace is mediated through the call of God that lifts us out of the ordinary and makes us instruments of God rather than creatures of sin. God's call conveys a grace that embraces the elect, not the world. Grace is the relief of being called out of bondage into the freedom of God's service.

Because vocation can be interpreted either collectively or personally it yields strong models with all four subjects. The called community of the Mormons, the Moonies of the Unification Church, and the Mennonites are as evident as the discipleship of individual marital martyrs. In all of them, however, there is a sense of willed distance from natural, accepted, and existing structures. Marriage is to be the creation of something different, not an adjustment to what is.

Because there is a greater gap between the gracious God and the natural world, the relation of marriage and faith is not as reciprocal as with sacrament. Here we have an almost exclusive focus on marriage as a symbol *of* faith but not as a metaphor *for* faith. The call proclaims God's willed initiative, which is to be brought to marriage in order to mold it to God's higher purposes. Marriage is the expression of God's call. Because it is tied so much to the world that is to be reconstructed, we are reluctant to draw on our experience of it for models for faith. This instrumental subordination of marriage to grace is, however, not necessarily a formula for church control over marriage. Persons and groups, as with the biblical prophets, can also exercise that discipline, because the call comes directly from God. The church exists more as chief respondent than as mediator of that call.

To find a heightened function for church, we must draw in the symbol of *covenant*. Here grace exists in the new community distinct from the world. Grace is manifested in certain patterns of human relationships. They are patterns flowing from the divine covenantal partner. In our table of covenantal models we can see that they are fairly evenly distributed along the axis from hierarchical household to egalitarian persons. All of them are characterized by a higher degree of voluntarism. Change and uniqueness are much more characteristic of these forms. The fact that they focus on relationships, however, makes them more applicable to families and households.

As expressions of willed initiatives, covenantal models are therefore more open to historical change. While sacramental models find their basis in nature as embraced by the church, and vocational models in nature as the object of God's mission, covenantal models find their "nature" in history—the events performed and remembered by communities. One of the reasons covenantal models appeal to us today is because of our heightened historical consciousness. They offer a source of dependable yet changing order.

Covenantal models therefore display a kind of selective reciprocity with faith. Marriage is seen as a symbolic model of faith in the sense that it mirrors forth the divinely manifested right order of relationships. On the other hand, since marriage itself is a profound relationship, it easily becomes a metaphorical model for the divine covenant. The story of Hosea expresses this reciprocity with great pathos and dramatic power.

What is important here is that the marriage that is to be a metaphor for faith is not necessarily the prevailing cultural norm. It springs from the wills of people of faith. It is exemplified in those marriages that exhibit a holy distinctiveness from the subverted

mores of our present culture. It is the singular fidelity of Hosea,
not the household authority of Everyman, that serves as the model
for faith. Therefore covenantal models are not as tightly bound to
institutional approaches to marriage. They can display greater
historical variability. Moreover, they direct our attention to the
unique ethical content of particular marriages rather than to marriage as an authoritative institutional form.

In emphasizing the priority of grace over nature, vocation and
covenant tend to reinforce the element of will. Marriage is an operation of our wills rather than the expression of our natures. Initiative is more important than adjustment. While this emphasis yields
a more dynamic conception of marriage it also can deny, repress,
and fatally distort our lives in the day-to-day process of loving. It
can come to treat the other person as an instrument and an object
in the moral project to which we have been called and for which we
have been covenanted. The symbols of vocation and covenant can
become a veil for willful exploitation in the name of unimpeacha-
ble higher authority. While they may have separated the church
out from the culture, they have trouble separating the will of God
from the will of the person—as spouse as well as parent.

Both vocational and covenantal models, while introducing a
more voluntaristic understanding of marriage, stress the divine initiation prior to human response. Their hierarchical thrust arises
not so much from appropriating cultural hierarchies as from
expressing the great gap between God and us. This subordination
is then expressed in psychological and social form. The ascetic
hierarchy of mind over body first seen in the sacramental approach
becomes that of will over feeling—the classic Puritan and Jansen-
ist preoccupations.

In rejecting the cultural accommodation implied by sacramental
approaches to nature, these symbols tend to reject nature altogether, thus making it difficult to engage persons as whole subjects
with dynamic natures. The question of whether "nature" may
refer to the constitution of individuals (as in personal models)
rather than of social orders (as in sacramental models) cannot be
addressed because the question of our natures has been sup-
pressed altogether.

The symbol that reopens a more naturalistic approach is *communion*. Here grace emerges in the persons as lovers. The bias of this symbol toward persons and couples is evident from the table. The resonance of two people creates the bond that leads people into such a sense of ultimate reality, confirmation, and acceptance that they can call it divine. The bond is based first of all on their natures—the constituent characteristics of their personalities—rather than their wills. It has a distinct character arising from this unique creation of the two as one. Grace is the power by which they make themselves fully present to each other so that the bond can occur and be nurtured. Grace is empowerment. It is known in the passionate reason of their fittingness for each other.

Communion, therefore, is experiential even before it is historical. Persons are distinguished from communities even as vocation and covenant distinguished communities from "the world." Communion stresses marriage as an experience of God's life rather than God's will or God's right order. It is a union of the affections rather than a discipline of the feelings or an agreement of reason. It is a participation in God before it is a following of Christ or a participation in the church.

All these characteristics dispose it to personal equality. While it stands at the opposite corner from sacramental tendencies toward household and family it shares with them a deep appreciation of nature. It defines nature personally rather than culturally, however. By focusing on persons it picks up the voluntaristic elements of human initiative found in vocation and covenant but without their preoccupation with will and behavior. People are seen more as free actors than as members of an authoritative cultural pattern.

It also shares with sacrament a greater reciprocity between faith and marriage. Marriages between lovers are metaphors for God's love. In the experience of peace and acceptance that they bring to us they also function as models of God's love. They are channels *of* God's grace as well as metaphors *for* talking about it. The communion version of this reciprocity differs from that in sacrament in that it has a personal focus. It is a providential achievement that cannot be generalized as a social rule or a pattern of law. The sacramental approach, in its tendency to embrace the world, takes on societal form much more easily. The degree to which this concern for worldly impact can be taken up in a communion approach will receive further attention below.

In general we can see that the meaning of nature and grace changes not only with each symbol but also with each model and subject. It is not enough to talk about nature and grace in general. For a theology of marriage we have to see that there are a variety of meanings these central terms can take on. Major landmarks in the marital landscape look different from different approaches. In any approach, however, we must try to find a proper interplay between nature and grace in our treatment of this "natural" phenomenon called marriage.

It is in our view of faith that we bring together the natural dynamics of our lives with the graciousness we experience from God. Faith binds us to that which we trust most. Our conception of ultimate trust inevitably shapes our approach to the bonds of trust at the heart of marriage and family life. With a consideration of this theological keystone we finish laying the foundations for our constructive theology.

Faith: The Trustworthy Relationship

Marriage is profoundly related to our understanding of faith. It is a matter of faith first of all because marriage forms a network of trust, whether between spouses or among family and household members. The demands of marriage press us to probe our deepest loyalties and resources for living. Marriage reveals our fundamental disposition to life, whether that be fear, trust, hatred, or resignation. It is a pattern of actions by which we make known that dependable commitment we call faithfulness. A theological view of marriage must inevitably turn to the meaning of marriage both as a revelation of faith and as a metaphor for understanding it.

Faith is action within a trustworthy relationship. It is participation in a fundamental bond. Each symbolic model bears a characteristic bond of faith. In sacramental models it is the bond with Jesus Christ as manifested in the church community. The common bond is the wider community held together in sacramental action. In covenant, the persons are bonded by the devotion to the primarily moral structure by which they are covenanted to God. Their bond springs from the mutual promises forming their communities and associations. With vocation the bond lies in the common calling experienced by the persons. It is realized in their common work as disciples. Finally, with communion, the bond lies in the one spirit permeating their lives. It is primarily an affective and emotional bond by which they are welded together "in the Spirit."

Faith is also the disposition we bring to participation in these fundamental bonds of trust. Our understanding of faith, indeed the very way we are faithful, takes a distinctive form within the bonds established by each symbolic model. In sacramental models faith emerges as participation in an embracing institution. It is a constant rehearsal of the symbols undergirding that social-ecclesial world. Faith is manifest in our membership in that wider cosmos. Faith is also evident in our trust in the established processes of that world. In its hierarchical forms this faith disposes us to sacrifice for the sake of that natural society enfolding us. In its organic and egalitarian manifestations, it emerges as a willingness to entrust our lives to a wider personal reality.

In vocational models faith is the disposition to obedience to God's call. Our lives are taken up in God's command, which rescues us from the confused wanderings of our normal existence and strengthens our will to act differently. To be faithful and to be "willed to God" are synonymous. We relate to others not immediately—that is, through their natures—but inter-mediately, that is, through God's call. To be faithful is to become a disciple and follow Christ. We trust in God's in-breaking demand rather than our own intuitions or our relationships with others, whether in church or in society.

Covenantal faith disposes us to responsiveness to a network of obligations and reciprocal claims. It is trust in the new world created by God's promises as well as our own. Faith emerges in the capacity to make promises and to keep them, even at great cost to other goods one may value. Faith is the trust that the one with whom we are covenanted is able to reciprocate and give us life for life in the covenantal bond.

In communion models faith emerges as the energy released by the conjunction of two souls in mutuality. Faith is the mutual affirmation arising in the union of kindred spirits. The discovery of our image in another disposes us to trust the underlying unity of life. This is something different from the sacramental trust of nature and the structure it connotes. It is a trust in life itself as an energy seeking actualization. Faith is being given over to the fire within, yielding up to it, abandoning our self-concern, and finding that the little pond of our fear empties into the great ocean of our birth.

Each of these forms of faith has its distinctive marks—*membership, discipleship, promise keeping,* and *empowering unity.*[9] Each has a distinctive way it incorporates features of hierarchy, organism, and equality, though with decidedly distinctive preferences. In each of these symbolic models faith is the way we struggle with the tension between self-concern and relationship with others. Faith is the way we deal with ourselves as beings in relationship—whether that be participation in a structured community, in single-minded discipleship, a network of promises, or the free dynamism of mutuality. Faith articulates our fundamental way of expressing ourselves and finding confirmation. In doing so it establishes the pattern of trust by which we can live.

All of these manifestations of faith make a legitimate claim on us. They are all valid ways of being faithful. We cannot be faithful in all these ways at once, however. Each era and context demands that we order these dynamics of faith so they find a fitting expression in a whole way of life.

The elements for engaging in this constructive effort have now been assembled—the symbols, the subjects, the models, and their manifold configurations and meanings. We have identified key values present in this rich harvest of faith experience. Out of this we can wrest a viable faith for our own time. That is the task for the next part.

NOTES

1. Psychoanalytic theorists stress these emotional bonds most of all. For a pioneer in developing systems theory in a Freudian framework, see Jules Henry, *Pathways to Madness* (New York: Random House, 1965), a study of five pathological families.

2. For the grounds for divorce, see Joseph Martos, *Doors to the Sacred: A Historical Introduction to Sacraments in the Catholic Church* (Garden City, N.Y.: Doubleday Image Books, 1982), chap. 11; Charles E.

Curran, "The Gospel and Culture: Christian Marriage and Divorce Today," in *Ministering to the Divorced Catholic,* ed. James J. Young (Ramsey, N.J.: Paulist Press, 1979), 15–36; and Lawrence G. Wrenn, ed., *Divorce and Remarriage in the Catholic Church* (Westminster, Md.: Newman Press, 1973). The behavioral dimensions are illuminated well in George Levinger and Oliver C. Moles, *Divorce and Separation: Context, Causes, and Consequences* (New York: Basic Books, 1979).

3. Richard Sennett is writing a four-volume series on "the emotional bonds of modern society," dealing with authority, fraternity, solitude, and ritual. In *Authority* (New York: Alfred A. Knopf, 1980) he argues that authority must take into account our fundamental need for nurture. Without this exchange between superior and inferior, periodic outbursts of rebellion will occur, as in strikes against paternalistic companies like Pullman and Kohler. His use of Hegel's model of the rise of consciousness from dependence to autonomy is similar to the transition we are charting here. For Hegel's views on marriage, see Rudolf Siebert, *Hegel's Concept of Marriage and the Family: The Origin of Subjective Freedom* (Washington, D.C.: University Press of America, 1979).

4. For the psychology of status and honor, see Julian Pitt-Rivers, *The Fate of Schechem, or the Politics of Sex: Essays in the Anthropology of the Mediterranean* (New York and Cambridge: Cambridge University Press, 1977), and Glen C. Dealy, *Public Man* (Amherst, Mass.: University of Massachusetts Press, 1977).

David C. McClelland is the dean of analysts of the psychology of achievement. See *The Achieving Society* (New York: Free Press, 1967).

The crucial role of identity, not merely as a stage in the life cycle but as a permanent concern for anyone in our culture, was formulated by Erik Erikson in *Childhood and Society* (2d ed. rev.; New York: W. W. Norton, 1963). See also "Identity and Uprootedness in Our Time," in *Insight and Responsibility* (New York: W. W. Norton, 1964), 81–108.

5. Anders Nygren, *Agape and Eros,* trans. Philip S. Watson (Philadelphia: Westminster Press, 1953), is the source for most discussions of this distinction, though he includes *nomos* (law) as the third motif rather than *philia.* Gene Outka emphasizes the patterns of mutuality in agape and struggles to reconcile it with friendship in *Agape* (New Haven, Conn.: Yale University Press, 1972). The thrust of my approach is more indebted to Paul Tillich. See *Love, Power, and Justice* (New York and London: Oxford University Press, 1960), and *Systematic Theology* (Chicago and London: University of Chicago Press, 1963), vol. 3, part 4, chap. 2, "The Spiritual Presence."

6. Marriages without intercourse or natural offspring had to be sacramental or else the Holy Family itself would not have been sacramental, a most perplexing conundrum. The problem of childless marriages has always been a tortured one, with radicals now appealing to it to justify intentional childless marriages "for the sake of the Kingdom." See

Dennis Doherty, "Childfree Marriage—A Theological View," *Chicago Studies* 18.2 (summer 1979):137–45.

7. The authority of the state to break up undesirable families is well entrenched. For a thoroughgoing analysis helpful to these reflections at many points, see W. Norton Grubb and Marvin Lazerson, *Broken Promises: How Americans Fail Their Children* (New York: Basic Books, 1982), esp. chaps. 2, 6, 7.

8. The institution of "no-fault" divorce in most states in the U.S.A. removes the dissolution of marriage from tort law altogether. The state, rather than having to adjudicate injuries and wrongs, simply controls the contract regarding division of property and custody of children. For an overview, see Riane T. Eisler, *Dissolution: No-Fault Divorce, Marriage, and the Future of Women* (New York: McGraw-Hill, 1977).

9. H. R. Niebuhr's discussion in *The Responsible Self* (New York: Harper & Row, 1963) lies behind these observations. People understand themselves with reference to a center of value which they apprehend in a variety of ways. See his essay, "The Center of Value," in *Radical Monotheism and Western Culture* (New York: Harper & Brothers, 1960), 101–13. Niebuhr's approach is foundational to James Fowler's view of faith (chap. 2 n. 4).

Faith as membership dominated earlier Roman Catholic discussions, as in Sebastiaan Tromp, *Corpus Christi Quod Est Ecclesia,* trans. Ann Condit (New York: Vantage Press, 1960), and Karl Rahner, "Membership of the Church According to the Teaching of Pius XII's Encyclical 'Mystici Corporis,'" in *Man in the Church,* trans. Karl-H. Kruger, *Theological Investigations* (New York: Seabury Press, 1963) 2:1–88.

Faith as discipleship is central to Dietrich Bonhoeffer's theology. See *The Cost of Discipleship,* trans. R. H. Fuller (2d ed. rev.; New York: Macmillan Co., 1966).

Jean Calvin's definition of faith as "a firm and certain knowledge of God's benevolence toward us, founded upon the truth of the freely given promise in Christ, both revealed to our minds and sealed upon our hearts through the Holy Spirit" (*Institutes,* book III, chap. 2, sec. 7) drew promising and promise keeping into the center of the life and thought of his spiritual descendants, whether as Puritan merchants or Scottish moral philosophers.

Faith as a kind of empowerment is typical of theologies emphasizing the Holy Spirit. For a christocentric approach, see Aaron Milavec, *To Empower as Jesus Did: Acquiring Spiritual Power Through Apprenticeship* (Lewiston, N. Y.: Edwin Mellen Press, 1982).

6

A Contemporary
Theology of Marriage

I have tried to show that marriage has many forms. These various models of marriage have been the vehicle for many social as well as personal purposes. Christians have associated a number of key symbols of faith with these forms of marriage. These faith symbols endow married life with a variety of deep religious meanings and purposes.

Over the past 150 years patterns of marriage have changed profoundly in most parts of the world. Some Christians try to retain the old forms and the way they were bearers of faith values. Others are searching for ways to affirm Christian faith in this new context. In different circumstances people could take the elements I have already discussed and erect different approaches to marriage. I cannot here lay out those responses to other situations. In this part I will set forth a Christian approach to marriage and family appropriate to the technological civilization typical of the North Atlantic countries. Many if not most of these features are already being lived out. This is one effort to give this expression of faith a coherent shape—a systematic theological form that can guide our lives, our ministry, and our approach to public policy.

This theological construction will begin with an affirmation of marriage as a natural pattern of relationships. The symbol of communion will be set at the center of our theological response to the nature of marriage in our time. Then the symbols of covenant, vocation, and sacrament will be woven around it to show how their perennial values are related to marital communion. I will conclude by showing some implications of this focus and way of ordering the key symbols.

MARRIAGE IS NATURAL

A Natural Metaphor for Faith

Marriage is above all part of God's created order. It is natural. It springs from the very way we human beings are constituted as affectional, active, rational, and social beings. It is an expression of who we are. As a reasonable observation this merely expresses the obvious claim that something called marriage has been central to all human cultures, even though its form has changed dramatically. As a theological statement of faith, it means that our dealing with marriage must first of all rest on a careful and sensitive understanding of who we are and what we are doing when we enter into marriage—not in some abstract sense but in the concrete everyday life of our own time and culture. From a faith standpoint, then, marriage is not primarily a project to be imprinted with our ethical and religious ideals but a way of living that has profound implications for the way we approach matters of faith.

Marriage is, first, a matter of nature, second a matter of grace. As a natural experience it can be a metaphor *for* faith in that it gives us vivid images for speaking about God's action. As a mine of rich metaphors for faith, marital and family experience helps us grasp and express the meaning of grace as *redemptive*—as the power of liberation and fulfillment. Our acceptance by the beloved betokens God's acceptance. Our parents' devotion to us mirrors God's faithfulness. The joy of sexual play anticipates the happiness of paradise.

Even as a natural phenomenon, however, marriage can also be seen as a means of grace. It can actually manifest grace in some way. As a symbol *of* faith, it is an expression of God's graciousness in the act of *creation.* In marriage we can come to sense more deeply the divine purposes infusing the created world. The confirmation of marriage and family is a form of God's blessing. The confrontations of family struggles are means of God's correction of our waywardness. In both cases, however, we begin with marriage as a lived reality and then move to its implications for faithful people.

Marital Nature:
From Substance to Action

The meaning of "human nature" has changed over the centuries from being a set pattern of relations, a substance so to speak, to being a capacity for transformative action. Our nature is not a static form to be filled out, but a set of rational and emotive capacities to pursue our purposes in a dynamic world.[1]

Therefore, to say that marriage is natural is not to say that it is a static legal form. We have a historical nature. Who we are depends on our role in a common history. We create our lives as a story in a wider drama. Our life is a social creation that emerges in our effort to present ourselves to others and to respond to their initiatives in confirmation and judgment.

People are essentially actors seeking expression and confirmation in a society by "going public" in a variety of appropriate settings. The problem of social life is how to establish and maintain these publics. The problem of personal life is how to cultivate the resources to enter that public sphere. Life in marriage, from this standpoint, emerges as a primary center for rehearsing our public lives. It is not private in the sense of being cut off from or opposed to public action. It is private in the sense of being deprived of both the heady praise and searching refinement of more objective audiences. Needless to say, this concept of our human nature challenges the preconceptions we generally hold about the character of public and private life. It also questions the view that we are essentially workers, laborers, servants, lords, or ladies.

Our human nature therefore revolves around our search for expression and confirmation among others. We seek to affirm the reality and worth of our life through interaction with other people. We seek a profound resonance with others that enhances our own energy and expands our powers beyond death and the negations of life.

Marriage as Communicative Union

In our own time this drive for publicity finds primary expression in a marriage where both partners have roughly equal powers—

economic, legal, and social. What happens in the marriage is a result of negotiation. Successful negotiation demands accurate and complete communication. It rests on a resonance between persons who can communicate on many levels, both tacit and explicit. Marriage becomes a communicative union of two people who can reveal themselves to each other and know they are received and understood. This view first emerged in the idea of "the companionate marriage." Now we say that marriage is a special kind of friendship.

This communicative union finds its first social expression in both partners' participation in the public spheres around them. Their life performs its symphony in the rhythm between intimacy and publicity. Indeed, the skills of intimacy—negotiation and communication—are also the skills necessary for public life. The household and children that may flow from the marriage are clearly subordinate to this primary axis. The children are not a precondition for expressing the drive for public life, whether by the mother or the father. They are "fruits of love" in the sense of being additional participants in the patterns of mutual confirmation in the little public of the household.

MARRIAGE AS COMMUNION

The Grace of Empowering Resonance

Among the four symbols that of communion has the greatest affinity for an egalitarian marriage. This is not to say the other symbols are irrelevant. It is merely to say that they are to be accommodated to the priority of this symbol and the values it bears.

In marital communion we find life as a process of resonance. Using the metaphors of physics, life appears as a constellation of electromagnetic fields, with levels of energy dependent on the relative harmony of the various wave patterns. The same dynamic of electric force known to physics has its analogous form in interpersonal relations. Here two beings create a whole new field of force out of the congruence of their own energy patterns. Likewise, this process emerges in the communication dynamics we know in public life, where mobilization, consensus building, negotiation, and testing either raise a people to new levels of power or plunge them into an entropic cycle of decline. With communion we have a master metaphor relating many areas of life.

What then does this symbol express about marriage? We have already seen that with regard to marriage as a matter of nature it lifts up the dynamics of resonant being. It focuses on the existence of a magnetic unity between two people that arises from who they are—from their being. Marriage arises from this union of being rather than from a complementarity of wills seeking to bring something new into the world—whether it is a family, a household, the Kingdom, or simply an ideal marriage. It is the experience of this resonant communion that then provides visions, images, values, and metaphors for faith and our understanding of God's gracious activity as Creator and Redeemer.

The image that communion provides for us as we seek to understand grace is empowerment. Communion is an excitation to higher levels of energy—a psychological equivalent of a cyclotron in which magnetic fields accelerate electrons for the purpose of splitting atoms. Communion is the way this cosmic creative power emerges in our life as actors in a field of human relationships. It is the divine power lifting us up out of torpor, fear, withdrawal, and death.

Communion lifts up the natural dynamics of birth, initiative, launching, vitality, growth, and change. While it brings the peace arising from intense mutual confirmation, it does not emphasize structure, endurance, and stability. Its "forever" springs more from a sense of depth than a promise of endurance. Communion connotes dynamic change rather than sheer permanence. Fidelity in this configuration rests more on intensity of attraction than on the rejection of distractions.[2] It means responsiveness to the partner more than control over the will. Neither covenanted longevity nor personal discipline is possible without the energy made available in resonant communion.

Similarly the entrance into this process is one of discernment rather than decision. It results more from an accurate sense about who the other person is than from a readiness to construct a common world of children and household. That is, it is a process of identification before it is one of commitment to membership or parenthood. Moreover, the actions of commitment are simply a publication of a union that has been discerned to exist between the persons. In short, communion is rooted in an emotional bond preceding acts of will and reason.

Conjugal Friendship:
The Model of Equality

Communion of this kind exists between people of equal personal power. Deep emotional bonds, of course, can and do exist between unequals, specifically between parent and child. Many intensely emotional marriages have really been a replication of this parental bond. The Trinity, as we saw earlier, has been a Christian symbolization of this marital model. Egalitarian communion, however, rests on a resonance of personal similarity rather than functional difference or dependence.

The egalitarian communion I am setting forth here differs from these other symbolic models in several respects. First, it is nourished by the powers the partners acquire through participation in public life—schools, churches, associations, corporations, and political parties. Their expectations and styles of action are molded by the experience of a public life that presses toward an assumption of equality. This equality is especially evident in the possession of knowledge and communication skills central to intimate life.

Second, the process of mutual confirmation is decisively reciprocal. Neither party is the final authority defining reality and right for the other. The authority for their life emerges in the communication that occurs between them. It is this communication process itself that is God's presence. Neither the man nor the woman is Christ's representative to the relationship. That presence is known only in the communicative spirit energizing their life.

Third, the social pattern they create is one of friendship rather than tutelage, service, or patronage. These acts of learning, helping, and care occur only as expressions of the experience of mutual enjoyment at the heart of friendship.

In distinguishing egalitarian communion from its hierarchical and organic counterparts we can also see how it reflects a kinship with politics and public life. While hierarchy mirrored the exigencies of military command and organicism the functional demands of economic production, equality is the precondition for a public life of reasonable persuasion. The personal capacities and disciplines for such a public life are lived and learned first of all in marital communion. Thus, communion, rather than being a retreat into privatism, represents a shift in priorities among economics, warfare, and politics. Marriage, rather than being a contract for householding and security, is a rehearsal for public expression and communication. Communion is indeed a private matter for couples, but its privacy nurtures a preparation for genuine public life.

In sum, marriage as communion focuses theologically on the Spirit, psychologically on expression and confirmation, and sociologically on public participation. Communion resides in the energizing power of the creative spirit. St. Paul notwithstanding, it is not to be linked first of all to Christ and his relation of authority to the church. The redemptive power and authority we associate with Christ resides firmly within the church rather than marriage. Second, marital communion has its social significance first of all in the way it prepares people for genuine public life rather than household maintenance and procreation.

Personal Identity in Communion

In the communion of two equal persons we bring together the values typical of communion, equality, and personalism. I need not repeat everything I said about them previously. My task here is simply to invoke them in order to show how they form an integrated ensemble.

The kind of personality evoked by communion in an egalitarian setting is characterized by a heightened capacity for expression through one's own body rather than through one's children, work, or possessions. This is the reason that we find such a stress here on integrating feeling and thought—a holistic model of the person.

The thrust toward expression is intrinsic to all human beings but has many forms. Our energy flows through the channels of our expression. They are the electric lines of our communication. Men have expressed themselves as makers, warriors, possessors, and administrators. Women, in being confined to expressing themselves through their children, necessarily used their bodies more for their expression. That is why many say they were "more in touch with their feelings." Because of the conditions of our social world, however, today both sexes must express themselves in direct communication with a vast variety of other people. This will always involve use of our bodies—first our mouth, face, and eyes, but then our hands, legs, and feet. Our whole body comes into play.

All of this is to say that self-disclosure stands at the center of healthy functioning. Moreover, this revelation of self is fairly unmediated by longstanding conventions of conversation and behavior. It is a creative disclosure of a unique self that constantly seeks to go beyond the typical messages and standardized expectations resident in established modes of communication.

This constant pressure toward the communication of unique experience further undermines standard conventions, thus requiring even more agile use of our whole body to convey our intentions and responses to others. Moreover, our alienation from the usual clichés of social life impels us to search for deeper experiences of resonance with someone who can affirm that we are indeed real. The search for confirmation and identity goes hand in hand with creative expressivity.

It is the capacity to construct our identity in the midst of confirming (and sometimes disconfirming) self-disclosure that gives us our self-esteem in life. This, rather than conformity to social expectations, gives us our sense of status. Our standing in the eyes of our marital partner constitutes the core of our self-esteem. Here it is not marriage itself, nor children nor household, that yields the rewards of status, but the sheer marital experience of confirmation.

Clearly this communion model does not primarily fulfill the broad societal purposes of children and security. Certainly children are not directly involved here. Neither is security, which the persons derive from their direct participation in the economy and civil order. The sole social purpose achieved through this marriage is that of psychological health. As I pointed out earlier, social institutions—businesses, associations, and governments—look to marriage primarily as a source of personal regeneration and empowerment. They have a great deal of interest in enabling persons to help each other grow in a marriage but no interest at all in keeping them together if these goals of personal health are not being met.

Indeed, they foster separation and divorce if this societal interest in fully functioning personalities is not being met.

Many churches today share in this societal perspective on the communion of the couple. They look to the couple primarily for the contribution their energized personalities can bring to the church public. They are concerned with the nurture of their communion in order to enhance their development as persons of faith. Churches do this in three ways.

Most important, they offer increasingly sophisticated counseling to enable people to discern the communion that must underlie an adequate marriage. This process of marriage preparation is not so much instruction or judgment as an opportunity for self-inventory and self-examination. It stimulates a process of discernment to enable the persons to see if the elements of communion are present.[3] Here churches have shifted from being institutional parents who can veto marriages to being counselors seeking to advance the growth of the persons.

Second, they seek to enrich the life of the couple—especially their capacity for communication. Marriage Encounter, Marriage Enrichment, and similar programs are typical means for this. These programs have lay leadership and provide arenas in which couples can try out new patterns of communication and receive encouragement from the group. The couples rather than the institution are in control.

Both of these thrusts are known through explicit, well-developed programs. The third means is less obvious. In light of the necessary tie between communion and politics, however, it is extremely important. Namely, churches provide the associational milieu in which people can learn and develop the skills of communication, negotiation, self-presentation, and understanding necessary in a marital communion. They gain a sense of being public persons in free association through their participation in running the church and its many organizations. This participation can be a source of self-esteem, confirmation, and identification with regard to an ultimate source of meaning. This kind of church experience can enhance the exercise of self that is then augmented in marital communion. This awareness of the church's impact on marriage in our time varies considerably from church to church. It is one that needs more articulation and systematic attention.

In all of these cases churches pursue the goal of nurturing personality development. Faith life focuses on the pilgrimage of the self through many stages of life—a self grounded directly in God and God's Spirit. The church then waits on the persons as individuals and as a couple to bring the fruits of their communion to a church assembly to enrich them in turn. The church is more a receiver than a mediator of the grace of marriage. For many churches this is a reversal of their earlier position, yet an inevitable outcome of the change I am reporting and advocating.

From Communion to Covenant

In this role of receptive nurturer the church affirms that marriage is a natural experience. It is grounded in God the Creator. Second, the church sees this communion as an experience that can provide metaphors for faith. People draw on their marital experience to help them express God's action in their lives. Marriage is not a means by which the church, as a redemptive association, expresses the faith it knows through its own history. Marriage is not an instrument of the church in that sense. This kind of marriage is an expression of the *creative* moment in God's action. It is an action preceding the church's faith. It is a field of primal experience that yields up metaphors for understanding the historical and public faith of the church.

Having established the centrality of communion, we can explore the ways other key symbols fill out its meaning and implication. Communion already exhibits a peculiar thrust to public life. How should we approach that theologically? There are social and ecclesial purposes that are not realized through marriage as couple communion. There is, indeed, even a certain incompleteness in communion's focus on depth rather than endurance. How can other symbols and models supplement it? Communion's need for some appropriate structure for articulating its power and energy presses it to appropriate the symbol of covenant.

COVENANTED COMMUNION

Persons who have entered into a profound communion seek to stabilize and structure the relationship that has given rise to this intense resonance. Covenant provides the form for maintaining communion. To understand this covenant and how it arises we must first examine its relationship to communion. We will then explore the ways the two classic forms of covenant—hierarchical and egalitarian—sustain two different embodiments of the marital communion.

We can recall from our earlier examination that covenant shares with communion an emphasis on the freedom and wills of the covenanted parties. This conjunction is the bridge between them. Communion is already rooted in the peculiar being of the two persons. They have established an energizing resonance because of this harmony of natures. While this communion is rooted in the very requirements of their being, it also is free of the wider necessities and obligations of life. In responding to this inner necessity that overpowers them, they also escape their normal ties to family, friends, work, and all other allegiances. They overcome the divisions of the world in the union of their love.

This dynamic of freedom is very threatening to social order. Societies have striven mightily to cage and control it. They have tried to impose an order on its oceanic currents. Sometimes they have called this structure a covenant or a contract. Institutions have provided compelling and authoritative structures in which this fire must be hearthed. But this imposed covenant is not the marital covenant flowing from communion. Though this marital covenant may draw on the formulations of past generations, it must rest on and draw its defining characteristics from the actual union of the two persons. While rooted in the necessity of their personal natures it also arises in the total freedom of their wills. The way these personal wills can be nurtured to construct a covenant appropriate to their communion will be dealt with when we discuss marriage as sacrament. At its center, however, marital covenant must rest on communion and draw its inspiration from it.

Covenant cannot produce communion, but only an external semblance of it. What it can produce is a network of promises in which the future is bound into the present and past. The present communion, with its cherished memories of fiery beginnings, is projected into the future through the commitment to maintain the conditions for its existence. The couple promise to honor the awesome field of magnetic attraction as the source of their new life in, with, and through each other.

In this free binding of the future we see the grace-full aspect of covenantal communion. Something new is being created, something that goes beyond what has been natural before. A new community is brought into being that can be seen and honored by others, and to which they can relate the other covenants binding them together. The communion becomes social flesh. It becomes incarnate in a world. Covenant provides the appropriate structure for communion. It redeems the future, with all its uncertainties and threats, for the sake of the new life that has arisen in the couple's midst. Here is the conjunction of the creative grace of communion with the redemptive grace of covenant.

Covenanted communion is rooted in the nature of the persons who have come together to form one flesh. Each couple has to generate the kind of covenant appropriate for embodying this union of souls. These covenants will take many forms. We cannot therefore specify all their elements. We can, however, distinguish the two major types of covenant that spring from marital communion—the marital and the parental. The distinction of these two types is crucial in our own time because of the actual separation of marriage from procreation. Let us first examine these two types of covenants before moving on to the manifestation of covenant in vocation and sacrament.

The Marital Covenant

This covenant has as its purpose the protection and preservation of the conditions for cherishing and nurturing marital communion. Covenant cannot produce communion. To claim this function for covenant would be to make marriage in essence into a moral project of redemptive will. Either one party will inevitably try to be the redeemer for the other, or the other will assign to him- or herself the role of sinful and stained victim. The person who is to be friend becomes a factor in a moral project whose excellence points to the divine status of the actor rather than to the field of beauty drawing the couple together. The covenant of marital communion must reflect the equality of the two persons in their commonality and similarity.

The meaning of marital covenant is thus shaped decisively by the egalitarian model bound up with marital communion. It is a covenantal form found only marginally in Scripture and then only between patriarchs. Indeed, covenant is not even related to marriage at all but to the welfare of the people. It is only when Hebrew covenant is translated into Latin, *pactum* ("compact, agreement"), that we pick up the egalitarian motifs of contract that have found full flower in our own time. The covenant of marital communion rests on this Latin background as well as the meaning that covenant took on in the congregational churches, where believers came together as equals in the Spirit to form a local church. In these two ecclesial traditions this marital covenant took on its egalitarian marital form.

In this structure of promises the flow of energy between the two lovers becomes a pattern of reciprocity and mutuality. The energy of their natural union now seeks to accommodate the natural interests that could divide them—money, children, decision making, relatives, and societal divisions. The entry into marriage must lift up not merely the conventional covenants offered to people by church and society, but the actual covenants by which they are to live in light of their unique history of obligations, strengths, weaknesses, and wants. Their informal and implicit covenant must be brought to life and examined in order to be ratified or modified.

To establish such a covenant demands communication and negotiation—the very potentialities already contained in communion. Here we find the personal values of expression and self-disclosure. The strength of the emotional bond is manifested in the degree to which the parties can give up their defenses in order to reveal the hidden edges of their natures and really receive the secrets of the other. The extent to which they have given themselves over to the emotional world that now energizes them is realized in the degree to which they can subordinate old ties to parents, friends, fantasies, work, and other emotional bonds. Marriages of communion have to become the central allegiance and covenant of their lives or they will be unable to bind together two free souls as friends.

This reordering of our emotional structures in covenanted communion demands that we return to our most primitive infantile bonds and transform them. We all think and act through the emotional patterns established to meet our deepest needs. Our primary bonds arise in the dependencies of infancy. In marital communion we find ourselves a new child in the field of play between us and our kindred soul. This mate emerges most clearly along the lines of brother-sister-friend, rather than parent-child. The discovery of communion in marriage is a recovery of our infantile life in its free form of play, that is, in our relations with siblings and friends. In this discovery we re-create the emotional patterns of our lives. We leave our infancy as son and daughter to gain a new childhood as husband and wife. Without this emotional restructuring we never "leave our father's house," as Genesis puts it, to become one flesh with our mate.[4]

The covenant built on this new birth must reflect the justice we know in childhood through games. It yields a structure of elementary fairness based on equality. The covenant is a structure of justice. It is the rules of our marital game. It exists so we might go on being equals in the enjoyment of our life together. Without it, the enormous power brought into existence by communion's fire can also burn undirected. We can become giddy with the pride that attributes our newfound power, self-esteem, and confidence to our selves rather than to our life together. We begin to go it alone and finally break the communion bond. The covenant must guard against our nature as egoists as well as protect our nature as friends.

Communion not only generates an emotional child-life. It also impels people to the generation of new flesh, product of their sexual communion. Egalitarian covenants give form to communion's emotional child. Hierarchical covenants give form to communion's physical child. This parental covenant has its own distinctive form.

The Parental Covenant

With the parental covenant we introduce the purposes of procreation and socialization. The companionship of communion expresses itself in the conception of new life. The energy released in the resonance of two bodies explodes in a sexual union whose process grips the essential fibers of ongoing being itself. A baby is born.

The relation of parent to child is essentially covenantal. This is even more evident in our own time when the birth of a child is a matter of conscious choice by the parents. It is an act of their wills. The distinction of the marital from the parental covenant gains greater clarity because of effective techniques of birth control, contraception, and abortion.

This element of choice and the distinction of the covenants has always been evident in the phenomenon of adoption.[5] Here we see the establishment of a fully invested parenthood, both emotionally and legally, as a completely free act of the parents. Indeed the power of this free parenthood has thrust it to the center of our image of God's parental care for Israel and the church. The parental covenant is a covenant of election, of chosenness. We are God's children by adoption, but we are no less God's children.

The parental covenant is clearly hierarchical. It is not the egalitarian covenant constructed out of the dynamism of communion. This covenant is established in parental initiative and infantile dependence. It is only as the children grow up that the model of their relationship can shift to an organic one of cooperation. In its fundamental form, however, parenthood is hierarchical. It rests in an inequality of status based on a disparity of strengths.

As I pointed out earlier it is the parental covenant that sees love as agape. It is the model for divine care. It is also the symbolic model most identified with God's covenanting in the Bible. Parenthood has been a pivotal metaphor for conceiving of God's relationship to us. It is a way of knowing God through our sense of absolute dependency. It has also been a primary expression of God's covenant. Through the actual exercise of parental rights and duties we have experienced divine power, authority, and care.

It is only because marriage in previous ages automatically entailed children that we have been unable to clarify this point. This is why the church's central faith concern has been oriented to procreation as the primary purpose of marriage. Now we can see that its desire to express faith focuses most appropriately on the parental rather than the marital covenant. This realization implies a fundamental shift in the church's whole orientation to marriage and family. Elucidation of this point is one of the central concerns of this book.

The parental covenant also exhibits other features found in bib-

lical covenant. First, it is the creation of a new community. The
marital relationship is more properly understood as a communion
than as a community. It does attain more of a visible communitar-
ian form in the marital covenant. The birth of a child, with the
creation of a whole new set of profound obligations, clearly manifests a new community. The creation of a new community is one of
the marks of covenant. With the birth of a child the couple has
created a family, a special kind of community. The parental covenant expresses this fact, so closely allied to the historical affirmations of God's covenant with Adam and Eve, with Abraham and
Sarah, with Israel in exodus, and with the church in Jesus' own
Passover.

Second, this covenant is more closely related to history than to
experience. Communion focuses on experience, covenant on history. With the introduction of a child into the world, a new generation begins. History, the succession of generations, steps forward.
A people maintain their life in time. The couple can, of course, participate in historic advance directly through their own public
action. Communion has an immediate relation with the public
realm as well as indirectly through children. But it is through the
creation of children that couples usually have bound themselves
into the advance of history.

Third, this covenant is formed by the initiative of one party—the
parents. In patriarchal times it was the initiative of the father. Intercourse and therefore conception was basically not dependent on
the consent of the woman. In our own time we are finally beginning
to reach the point where marriage is not a respectable form of sexual slavery. Conception and birth are not only a matter of the
woman's initiative, but also a result of joint deliberation and
responsibility. In establishing the parental covenant the parents
act as one party. This is a model of divine initiation in the affairs of
history. The covenant is initiated from above.

Fourth, this covenant is an imposed covenant. The conditions
are established by the parents. While children learn early on how
to begin rewriting this covenant, its basic form is imposed on them.
Not only is it ordained by the parents. It is also ordained by the
society, which is primarily concerned with children and their proper
socialization. Many institutions constrain the parents to their vari-

ous responsibilities for their offspring. In bringing children into the world the parents enter into a covenant whose conditions arise not from their own wills but from the needs of wider communities.

Finally, the parental covenant understands fidelity in terms of duration, permanence, and perseverance. A covenant is a promissory relationship. The birth of a child brings this into full relief, for a child is not merely an immediate actor in the covenant. A child is eighteen years of responsibility at the same time that he or she is an immediate obligation. Children are in themselves a bundle of promises. Parents are bound in with them at least until they are mature. The trajectory of parenthood extends beyond that even to death. The parental covenant is the actual locus of fidelity as permanence. The parent-child bond is unbreakable in a way the marital bond is not.

This peculiar character of parental fidelity can exist because the relationship is covenantal. It is the product of will. It is an act of grace brought *to* our existence. It can constantly be renewed by the efforts of one of the parties—principally the initiating party. Even when one party breaks the covenant, the other can continue to act in accord with it. This is the testimony of Israel and the church. Here again we find the harmony between the parental and biblical covenants.

This act of continuing fidelity springing from the initiating will of the superior party is quite different from that arising in communion. With communion, the marital covenant arises out of the energy of the two persons coming together in an amazing harmony of being. If the harmonic source of their energizing communion is ever extinguished there is nothing one party alone can do to re-create it. It depends in its essence on the presence of both. The parental covenant, on the other hand, arises from the wills of persons who exist prior to the child. It is something they can constantly seek to re-create. It exists as long as they will it.

This characteristic of permanence also depends on the fact that the parents are originally more powerful than the child. They are stronger, or wealthier, or more socially secure. In this sense, to put it bluntly, they have leverage with the child. The permanence of the covenant is an expression of their relative power. To the degree that the child gains an equality or even dominance in their power balance, the original parental covenant becomes more difficult to sustain. It usually takes on a more organic model in which execution of family tasks replaces subservience to status prerogatives.

Thus, the difference between the marital and parental covenants depends heavily on the difference between the egalitarian model typical of spousal interaction and the hierarchical model congenial to parenting, with the familial organic model characterizing the later years of parenting. The differences between these two patterns of relationships help us understand more precisely the significance of the theological distinction between the biblical parental covenant and the ecstatic communion covenant. In order to grasp this distinction more completely, let us turn once again to an analysis of the emotional bonds holding the two covenants together.

In its main features the parental covenant is not a matter of communion. In previous times many of the dynamics of communion often did occur between parents and children. The emotional needs to be served in marital communion were displaced to the children because the marriage relationship itself was a relationship of unequals. Wives mothered their husbands and husbands were fathers to their wives. The marriage was simply a replication of the parental relationship. By seeking to establish the emotional bonds of communion with children, parents set up a psychological pattern in them that would ensure that they too would re-create the same relation in the next generation. From the standpoint of achieving conjugal friendship, this was an immense and crippling confusion.

Earlier I pointed out how the egalitarian model presses toward the value of *personal identity*. In its communion form this identity arises in the intense dynamism of expression and confirmation between the spouses. The hierarchical model lifts up the value of *parental status*. Here our emotions are tied up in acting out a status position, in this case of mother and father. Our psychological need for expression and confirmation revolves around establishment and maintenance of the parental status gained by rearing children.

When marriage and parenting were fused together, our identity was welded to our parental status as householders. Until the mid-nineteenth century only men of property (that is, owners of households) could vote. The public action of women was legitimate only as an extension of their maternal status. People had identities as public actors only to the extent they had a parental or household status.

This fusion has largely dissolved. Today we can have identities as public actors without a parental, household, or even marital status. Friendship, especially marital friendship, itself is an emotional base for forming an identity that can create the strength necessary for public life. Possession of the status of patriarch, matriarch, mother, or father is not enough to confirm us emotionally or enable us to gain entree to the wider public.

This public action is something we do. It is an achievement entailing the risk of failure. It yields opportunities for intense expression and confirmation, but it lacks the security that comes from simple possession of a status. Possession of a status like parent or child arises simply from who we are. Raising children offers a different mode of expression as well as of confirmation. Children do not have the same power to confirm us that a spouse does. They cannot and ought not be mirrors of us. Nor can they be friends or lovers. In being covenanted with children, parents do not seek the values found in communion. Their identity and capacity to act in society does not depend on their children.

This means that parental covenant produces a parental disposition that is more professional. It is the exercise of a status and duties that devolve finally from God's purposes. This stance moves us away from the kind of emotional relations that have been advanced in recent decades and recalls the more detached, but no less serious and loving, stance of the Puritan parents, for whom parenthood was part of their covenantal relation with God.[6]

Not only does this covenantal approach relieve parents of some of the emotional manipulation typical of recent generations. It also may help them see more clearly that parenting is not merely an aspect of the private relationship of marriage, but also a dimension of the common and public action of raising up a new generation of people. We will return to this later with the symbol of vocation.

The distinctiveness of the parental covenant may also help children become emotionally freer to find innovation in their own marriages rather than replicate the quasi-communion bonds they had with their parents. They are thus freer to establish with sibs and friends the bonds that can become the emotional paradigms for marital communion. They can differentiate themselves, as systems theorists like Salvador Minuchin would say, from their family of origin in order to participate in a genuine marital partnership.[7]

In previous ages, I might add, especially because of higher infant mortality, parents were often able to have a more covenantal bond with their children. They belonged first of all to God and to the community for whatever time, long or short, they were in the world. Large families probably also fostered more possibilities for sib bonds, although younger children probably saw older siblings as parental figures. Thus, we should not be surprised that genuine marital communion has been known at all times, even through generational lines. Because of the almost universal subordination of women, however, this was very hard to achieve or maintain. Communion bonds were usually displaced to same-sex friends and sibs, or realized in various forms of mystical communion.

To say that children are once removed from the relationship of communion is not to say that there are no emotional bonds between them and their parents. It is simply that the emotional structure is different and serves different psychological needs. They are clearly not so distant from parents as to become mere property. They are members of a family, not merely parts of a household. As participants in a covenant they have the status of persons, though they have yet to exercise all the faculties of personhood in the society.

It is important to stress this distinction between family and household, because children have, like women, often been treated as types of property in the law of earlier generations. Children are the products of our bodily interiors and not merely our hands. Children grow up. Possessions do not. Children respond with increasing linguistic facility. Possessions do not. They are actors, not props, in the drama of our private life.

This distinction is very important because in cases of divorce children have usually been treated as aspects of the household or as things to be owned by one or the other parent. By clarifying the marital and parental covenant we see that the breakdown of the one need not entail the breakdown of the other. Christians should seek to make sure that they do not. In treating children as a species of property we have failed to honor the parental covenant by maintaining as best we can the bonds between children and both of their parents.[8] This is an important societal consequence of our clarification of the parental covenant.

We can now see that the exercise of parenthood as covenantal obligation draws us out of the private relation of the couple and into the public sphere inhabited by parents with common interests to pursue. Here their common status as parents draws them together for the sake of their children—children to whom they have *common* obligations. Parenthood is a public status embedded in a web of relations with one's people.

In this movement toward the public sphere we come to the boundary between the parental covenant and the wider social and ecclesial covenants that it implies. The marital communion produces not only a marital and parental covenant. It also yields a social and ecclesial covenant, whether through the public action of the couple or their creation of children. The society enters into covenant with the couple through its primary concern for the raising of children. The church community, already having received the graces of new life from the energy of the couple's communion, now enters into a covenant with them as parents—a covenant resonant with the church's own covenant with God.

To understand the meaning of these two covenants we are actually led to the other two primary marital symbols—vocation and sacrament. It is in the light of vocation that we work out the societal covenant. Through the symbol of sacrament we express the meaning of this ecclesial covenant.

MARITAL VOCATION:
THE SOCIETAL COVENANT

To have a vocation is to have a calling. It is to be called out by a power and purpose beyond ourselves. In this calling out from life-as-usual we find immediate evidence of vocation's tension with nature. It is a thrust toward that which is not yet. It is a lure toward the unique new life God intends for us. It is anchored in God's redemptive purpose.

Yet our call is also rooted in certain dynamics and tendencies within us as human beings. It does have a grip on the way we are created and constituted. It is also an implication of our natures. Its point of entry into our ordinary experience lies in our drive toward *publicity*—a life of more expansive expression and confirmation. That is, vocation is the theological approach to our own need and desire to express our lives in some kind of public world where others can confirm our existence and where we can find a real if limited affirmation of our worth and power.

In short, the divine call emerges from the perfect publicity of God's republic. It arises out of the glory of the perfect confirmation and affirmation possible in God's realm. We are drawn out of our isolation and chaotic wandering by the ultimate power of this perfect public. But this attraction appeals to the deepest drive of our being—the drive to present ourselves before others in mutual acts of confirmation. It is this reality that we already taste in the experience of communion and that we seek to articulate in covenant.

The idea of vocation expresses our sense of being called out of the darkness of unreality—out of our isolated imagination, fears, fantasies, and illusions into the confirmation possible in argument and discussion with others. Communion, even though intense and energizing in itself, seeks to augment itself in a wider public at the same time that it seeks to express its remarkable good news to the world.[9] Vocation expresses our movement out of the intimate darkness into the public light. The delicate yet intense laser of love seeks more comprehensive expression in the public eye.

The symbol of vocation stands at the center of the process by which we express ourselves in a worldly history. It is the hands of our covenantal body gripping the tough fabric of human affairs. Vocation provides the arena for professing the significance of our lives as people who have been energized in communion and accounted for in covenant. This is the personal depth of vocation, leading us from intimate communion and personal responsibility to social activity.

Vocation, then, is the invitation to establish and participate in a public world. There are two aspects to this activity—*innovative* and *ordering*. The innovative work of vocation points to its redemptive purpose rooted in God's new creation. The ordering work honors the graciousness God extends to us in the present patterns of social life.[10]

Vocation emerges as an expression of the new life that has arisen in marital communion. A sense of vocation of course can arise out of other experiences of intense communion with God and creation. We are here directing our attention to understanding vocation in the marital context. In communion persons have gained a new identity in bringing to expression the deepest levels of their own being. The crust of parental and social expectation has broken away under the impact of the harmonic resonance that has emerged between truly kindred souls. It is this new identity that now seeks worldly expression. It seeks to make a profession of itself. Inasmuch as this new being is utterly unique it will seek to create a new world that can bear forth and confirm this new way of life. The love that has renewed the persons seeks to spread out and renew the earth. This is the redemptive and innovative impact of marital covenant.

The symbol of vocation also underlies the orderly disposition of our energies within the present social order. Vocation is not only a call to create a new world. It is also a call to take up a specific role in the wider sweep of God's renewal of creation. The work of divine salvation is not entirely in our hands. Each of us has a unique role to play in this cosmic drama. Our ultimate confirmation does not lie in shaping every aspect of the universe to accord with our own sense of new life. We are to express this new being in a theater appropriate to our own history, culture, age, and abilities. Vocation is therefore a call to be faithful in a specific place, time, and activity rather than to exhaust and dissipate our energies in a frenetic effort to do everything at once.

Both of these aspects are important. To emphasize only the first is to deny our natural rootedness and limitation. To invoke only the second leads to the danger of simply accommodating to the old order of things and not being faithful to the impulse to new life arising from our marital communion and covenant.

Because of the natural character of marriage, it has tended to drift toward the pole of vocational order and social adaptation. The marital vocation has been seen as the call to maintain the established social order. Marriage as a calling has served the societal purposes of security and children. The calling of marriage was expressed centrally and almost exclusively in procreation. In this approach the newness of life emerging from marital communion was then directed toward having children and preparing them for entry into the existing occupational order.

In that situation the innovative and redemptive thrust of vocation was displaced from the couple almost entirely and was placed solely on unmarried individuals. Redemptive vocation cultivated an individualism epitomized in the image of the saint. For many centuries of course the claim that vocation had anything at all to do with marriage was simply denied. Reformation churches reintroduced the concept of vocation into the natural life of marriage, but with a decisive compromise. The man exercised the creative and innovative side of vocation, while the natural and ordering aspect was expressed through the procreation assigned to the woman. In the nineteenth century this eventuated in the concept of the "two spheres"—one for the woman in the home, the other for the man in the public sphere. The two aspects of vocation were split from each other in accord with the hierarchical and organic models of marriage. Only in isolated cases such as that of the missionary couple was this sense of joint vocation preserved.

As Carl Degler has pointed out, this division of spheres at least gave women some sense of having a redemptive vocation—if only in bearing and raising children. They expressed new life in its most dramatic form—the baby. But they were barred from the renewal of the public order, whether in occupations or politics. When they finally did enter the public realm it was to maintain the sanctity and security of the home.

With the two spheres women had to choose between exercising their "natural" vocation as mothers and their innovative vocation as professionals in the public realm. Most became mothers, some became professionals, and a tiny remnant did both. In the first half of this century more and more women tried to do both. Men increasingly shared in cooperative decisions about parenthood. First, they agreed to negotiate the planning of fewer births. Then they began to share more fully in the process of parenting itself. We are now coming to the point where the egalitarian impulse of communion is expressing itself more fully in the vocation of the couple as equal partners in parenthood. The vocation of marriage has been reshaped by the rise of communion as the central marital symbol.

Even with this emergent pattern, however, the marital vocation is channeled almost exclusively through the creation of a family. The vocation of the couple is confined to their call to raise children. There are two problems in this, one theological, the other social.

Theologically, this approach neglects the direct public significance of the couple and their new life. The creative, innovative, and redemptive actions of the couple in occupational and public life are neglected or denied altogether. The fullness of the meaning of vocation is constricted or denied. A public vocation is restricted to the persons rather than being tied to the couple.

Socially, we still have a pattern in which the woman seeks a wider public life at the same time that she still carries all the major burdens of raising the children and maintaining the household. Because of this, women systematically are deprived of an equal participation in the public sphere—both occupational and political. The major obstacle to an equal sharing in parenthood and in public profession is the structure of occupational life. No advance will be made toward a fuller expression of marital vocation until we change our patterns of jobs, careers, and work processes. Not only do we need to press for more flexible work schedules, greater use of electronic means of communication to connect home base with work place, and infant-care arrangements, but also opportunities for couples actually to share work, occupation, and career as the expression of their common identity.[11]

Our present economy reflects an individualistic sense of vocation. Marriage as communion drives toward a concept of joint vocation. The sharing of parenthood will be incomplete until we actively support the sharing of vocation in its fullest sense. When both are accomplished we will have come closer to honoring not only the egalitarian impulses of communion but also the full integrity of vocation as public profession and renewal as well as procreative expression and replenishment.

This then is the structure of building a world based in marital communion. Vocation, however, is not only bound to social life in general. It is not only a calling out into the public. It also lies at the root of our concept of the church. The Greek word for church, *ekklesia,* comes from the word which means "called out." The church is also a peculiar way of life for those called out. It is a special vocational form. As such it has a special tie to marriage as a vocation. In pressing this connection, we move more fully into the light cast by the symbol of sacrament.

CHURCH AS SACRAMENT OF
MARITAL VOCATION

The central theological meaning of marriage and family is constituted by an ensemble of four symbols. We have traced the implications of placing communion at the center of marriage by showing how it develops in covenant and vocation. In this development we have seen how the primacy of nature in communion passes to the importance of grace in vocation. We have moved from marriage as a *metaphor for* understanding God's grace to marriage as a *manifestation of* God's redemptive purposes in re-creating our world.

This way of ordering the key symbols has been deeply conditioned by the nature of society in our own time—increasing life span, availability of birth control, equality of the spouses, and the centrality of communications. This configuration is also shaped by the conviction that people are beings who seek ever fuller publicity to establish the reality of their lives. Our search for salvation is expressed in our desire for a more perfect public in which we can profess our lives in action before others and respond to their professions in turn. This search for a perfect republic is our modern version of the quest for the Kingdom of God.

In order to understand the peculiar role of the church within the dynamics generated by marital communion, we have to remember the importance of this thrust for perfect publicity. Second, we have to remember that the church is primarily concerned with the redemptive thrust of God's grace. In relating to marriage the church must focus first on the announcement and cultivation of this perfect realm presided over by God. Its first task is to see how this realm can be advanced through witness and public action. Second, it needs to see how the natural fact of marital communion can advance this anticipated Republic of God.

With the concept of sacrament we come to a central exercise of the church's responsibility for advancing God's perfect public. To understand how sacrament cultivates this realization of God's governance we must first clarify our understanding of the dynamics of sacramental action.

Ritual action stands at the center of the conception of sacrament I am working with here.[12] A sacrament is a symbolic ritual action. It is ritual in that it has a definite pattern of action established by tradition. It links us to past communities. It is symbolic in that it brings vividly into our life a vastly wider pattern of associations, expectations, understandings, and emotional dispositions. It is action in that we move as well as are moved. It is a dramatic form. It is a dramatic nucleus of a wider public performance. Sacramental action provides essential patterns of meaning for acting in the drama of birth, commitment, failure, death, and renewal. Sacraments are rehearsals for life.

Sacramental action therefore constitutes the cultural core of meanings, values, and enlivening motivations for professing our life. It is an activity bringing together action, thought, and emotion, binding together not only persons but also publics of various sizes. Sacraments frequently tend to become fixed on the past and its ossified behaviors. At that point they lose their redemptive grace as a rehearsal for God's ultimate public. They need not only memory and present consensus to have meaning. They also need to cultivate new forms of profession in light of the Spirit of God's emerging world. It is because of their preparatory enlivening that sacraments can be occasions of redemptive grace. It is in building the cultural matrix for a more perfect public that they are the internal action of a people who have been called out of the present privations of their lives.

In its sacramental action, therefore, the church is a "proleptic public." It is a partial realization of the more perfect public we long for. In sacramental action the church seeks to build up the base of common meanings, action patterns, and dispositions that make possible communication in a wider public.

In turning to marriage and family the church seeks ways that this natural reality can evidence this thrust toward salvation. How can these human relationships become expressions of this working of grace? Marital communion already energizes adults who can

bring their gifts to the communities and institutions of the church.
How can these structures in turn advance God's redemption
through the patterns of marriage, family, and household?

In general churches should provide the primary cultural arena
in which couples, families, and households can profess their new
life in a world-transforming way. They can do this in two ways, the
first regarding the covenant of parenthood, the second regarding
the vocation of the couple.

First, they provide a primary community in which children can
be raised in awareness of God's redemptive purposes. Just as the
biblical covenant is first of all a parental covenant, so is the
church's sacramental action first of all concerned with parenthood,
not spousal union. The communion of the couple is grounded in
nature. The exercise of their parenthood participates in and is to
be shaped by the community living in anticipation of the new
world. Children are an earnest reminder of that newness and frequently are an expression of the couple's faith in the future. The
church, as a sacramental cultivator of more perfect publicity, is primarily interested in rehearsing emergent persons for the drama of
faithful living.

Ironically, this revives and even intensifies an earlier church
claim that procreation took precedence over companionship as the
purpose of marriage. Now we can see, however, that these two purposes have different social subjects. It should be clear by now that
the unity of marriage and procreation brought about a preoccupation with the events of the wedding rather than the birth of the
child. Now that couple communion has emerged with its own integrity and independence, we can see more clearly the significance of
directing church concern to parenthood as such. *Here lies the sacrament.* The church can only receive the gifts of the couple as a
kind of "natural sacrament" of love, but it has a redemptive
responsibility to advance children toward a life of profession and
publicity.

We might note that infant baptism fulfilled this sacramental role
in earlier times. It was equated more with entrance into the church
community than into the Kingdom as such, but it did give public
recognition to the child. Under the impact of the reordering I am
advocating here, the sacrament of marriage would be replaced by

the sacrament of parenthood. Baptism as a sacramental action would occur when the developing person wished to become a responsible member of the church as a public assembly. Confirmation would refer to subsequent intensification of this commitment in times of revival and deepening conversion.

By placing the sacrament at the point of parenthood, that is, the creation of a family, the church reflects more clearly the values of biblical covenant. It also sets forth more clearly its concern for the renewal of the public world. Finally, the sense of hierarchical tutelage that we associate with the church's sacramental action finds a more appropriate place in reference to child development than to adult profession.

As we saw earlier, sacramental models have tended to focus on the family and household. This is true of sacrament even in this configuration. The work of salvation is a work of enhanced publicity and confirmation. A family develops this in its household life. This household life, however, is not an isolated world but a foyer into a wider public. The church, in its sacramental life, needs to enable the household to be a hospitable though limited public in which people can rehearse their public lives. The household is more a little theater than a refuge, a dress rehearsal than a retreat. Church effort to support such a household life, especially for the sake of the children, leads us to the second way that churches can relate to marriage sacramentally.

The church's primary sacramental attention should be directed at the sacrament of parenthood, but it also needs to reclaim the sacramental core of the public vocation of persons and the couples they constitute. If marriage itself is still to be taken seriously as some kind of sacramental reality, we have to turn not merely to the exercise of parenthood but to the equally important expression of the couple in professing a vocation. Vocational profession and covenantal parenthood are the twin expressions of marital communion. They both deserve appropriate attention from the church.

In pointing out the difficulties faced by efforts to take marriage seriously as a Christian vocation, I pointed out the need for reform of occupations, careers, and workplaces. Without these economic changes we will not be able to enable both partners in marriage to profess themselves fully in public life. This economic reordering therefore becomes an important task of churches as vocational communities.

Their contribution to this task as sacramental communities is to lift up the commitment to a vocation as a core act of Christian faith—that is, as sacrament. Our entry into a public discipline in response to God's call needs to be celebrated and supported by the church. This pursuit of a vocation is central to our witness to God's redemptive purposes. In a ritual profession of this response we legitimate its centrality and the claims it makes on us. Moreover, in seeing this life in vocation more sacramentally, the churches also commit themselves to a sustained critique of all narrow occupationalism and shallow careerism that degrades the divine republic which vocation serves.

Over the centuries Christians have tried to find a sacramental response to vocation, first in monastic life and then in clerical ordination. There it has frequently been used to legitimate a constriction of the call to wider publicity. In our own time more and more Christians have rediscovered the general meaning of the vocation of the Christian public. Now we can begin to refocus sacramental action around response to this general call. With regard to marriage we need to give an important place to the call of the couple to pursue a joint vocation.

An elaborate ritual tradition lies behind the vows to religious profession, though only in the case of priestly ordination has this gained the status of a sacrament as such. Movement toward a sacrament of vocation would draw our understanding away from these priestly and monastic forms and link it more closely to its baptismal roots. This would be a very appropriate move for two reasons. First, the idea of the call orginally devolved on a whole people, not a leadership elite. A closer tie between vocation and marriage helps keep vocation oriented toward the task of the whole people of God, most of whom are married. Second, people's eligibility for marriage has consistently been linked to their status as baptized Christians rather than to any higher evidence of response to a special call. By linking marriage and vocation more closely and identifying a variety of ways this marital vocation can be exercised we help remove the elitist and individualistic elements it gained through its long priestly, monastic, and Puritan development.

In providing the symbols for understanding, legitimating, and expressing our lives in marital vocation, churches take seriously the primacy of couple communion as a free natural gift emerging from our creation. They appropriately address their redemptive and world-transforming concerns to the parental and other public expressions of this communion. In sacramental action they not only lift up symbols that unite people in mutual confirmation. In providing the symbolic resources for public life they empower people to become whole persons capable of communion. They provide deeply interior symbols that can help order our basic emotions and dispositions. Through the vividness of symbolic action they weld our emotions into a pattern of willing that makes it possible to translate communion into covenant. Moreover, in expressing common symbols they embed in us the very images, ideas, and ways of being that underlie the possibility of communion itself. Sacramental action undergirds our personalities as well as our public world.

Sacramental action not only helps establish the psychological conditions and cultural bonds that make it possible for two people to enter into communion with one another. It also calls us out to a wider identity. It provides in baptism an understanding of ourselves as equal citizens of God's public. In vocation it confirms us as actors in response to God and others, empowered to profess our own life, confess a common life with others, and engage in the conversation of living.

In observing this dynamic we see how the ensemble of symbols makes a full circle, each symbol reinforcing the others in particular ways. Communion finds structure in covenant. Covenanted communion finds expression in parenthood and vocation. The efforts to express this essential communion find form and grounding in sacrament. This grounding in turn can create the means of communication that make communion possible. This is how we can grasp these symbols as a coherent constellation to guide a faithful navigation of the terrain of marriage and family in our time.

CONTEMPORARY MARRIAGE AND FAMILY: PROSPECT AND PRACTICE

I have now provided a framework for approaching marriage and family as a matter of faith. This framework rests to some extent on convictions about God, the church, and human life that cannot be fully argued in this short book. At least the underlying ideas of expression, confirmation, and publicity should have become familiar and understandable in the course of our exploration. They constitute the human nature a theology of marriage and family must engage. In marital life people have increasingly differentiated their actions as persons, couples, families, and households. They enact at least three patterns of relationships. This is the sociological nature of marriage and family today. Finally, the symbols of sacrament, covenant, vocation, and communion point to the enduring principles and values that Christians should seek in personal, marital, familial, and household life. An adequate theology must take account of all of them.

The basic structure of a contemporary Christian approach to marriage and family should now be clearly visible. In some cases the changes are dramatic. Communion reshapes covenant, vocation, and sacrament in challenging ways. The core of marital communion gives rise to both a marital and a parental covenant. The couple find their call not only in parenthood but also in direct public action. The sacramental concerns of the church are fastened clearly to the covenantal and vocational expression of the couple rather than to their bond itself. The sacrament of marriage is transformed into the sacraments of parenthood and public vocation.

In other cases the outcomes are consolidations of recognized conditions. Marriage is seen first of all as a companionship of equals. Childbearing is distinct from the marital bond. Families may be structured among households in a variety of ways. Moreover, the spouses participate directly in public and occupational life as well as through their household.

This is the prospect that emerges in our reconstruction. To see some of the practical challenges this entails let us turn to the four areas of personal nurture, weddings, and the two professions of parental and public vocation.

Personal Nurture

Individuals need nurture, support, and counsel as they make their way in their increasingly complex relationships. The motives of expression and confirmation can help guide us to practices appropriate to this personal venture. Two activities need our attention—pastoral counseling and church administration.

Pastoral counseling has become a sophisticated and demanding part of pastoral action. Ministers are trained in many approaches—Jungian analysis, rational-emotive therapy, Rogerian counseling, transactional analysis, and systems therapies, to name only a few.[13] The thrust of this essay is to ask us to evaluate how these practices cohere with the motives of publicity informing the dynamics of communion. Moreover, it asks us to pay attention to which subject they appropriately apply.

The fulfillment psychologies of Carl Rogers and Abraham Maslow, for instance, are very appropriate for people's needs for expression. The more rational therapies, such as those of Albert Ellis, help get at inadequate patterns of confirmation. They help us to analyze and reconstruct crazy mental worlds that arise as we engage in mutual confirmation with others. Depth analysis helps persons and couples unlock their emotional bonds with their families of origin in order to gain greater individuation, thus enhancing their own capacities for communion. Finally, the behavioral and systems therapies are most appropriate for reorganizing destructive family and household patterns.

Counselors need to think through the appropriate approach to each situation in light of what subject is the focus of concern. Awareness of the constellation of possible patterns set forth in chapter four can help counselors discern what kind of marital and familial world people are coming out of. Are they rooted in a vocational or a sacramental orientation? Is the couple or the family central to their marriage? Which model of relationship are they presupposing? Before seeking any change the counselor must understand their marital world. Then possibilities for change can be assessed by looking at the typical relationships among the approaches as they emerged in chapters five and six. People with a hierarchical sacramentality can be invited to explore the possibilities of organic covenant. People tied solely to egalitarian communion can be led to its implications in covenant and vocation. Thus spiritual and psychological change can proceed in steps appropriate to the persons' starting points.

The second and more neglected area of pastoral concern regards the way the public life of the church affects people's growth as communicators and negotiators.[14] Pastors need to take account of the personal impact of the processes of decision making and implementation in the church. Are meetings opportunities to enhance our ability to express ourselves, listen to others, negotiate, reach consensus, and confirm the participation of others? Are ministers at least as attentive to the nurture of the participants as they are to arriving at the "right" conclusion? Do patterns of church participation contribute to appropriate individuation by older children? Do they provide opportunities for couples to work together rather than as divisible cogs in a smoothly oiled machine? Is there provision for developing skills in communication among singles as well as couples? These are some of the questions we must address to bring the public life of the church into line with personal patterns in marriage and families.

Weddings

Churches should be less involved in weddings, especially as sacramental moments. Their concerns should fall first of all on the lifelong nurture of persons of faith. The wedding is an opportunity to do that, but the act of getting married is not the appropriate focus of its concern. This concern should be devoted to the process of personal inventory and covenant making. What does this mean?

Many churches have already become committed to an obligatory practice of premarital counseling. It works best when practiced as a process of discernment to see whether people are ready to exercise the skills of marital intimacy and also to help them see if true marital communion exists between them. This is extremely salutary. It should be extended in time so that it becomes an ongoing spiritual discipline outside as well as within marriage.

This process of discernment before people publish their bond in the wedding ceremony should lead to the construction of the marital covenant. Drawing on the images at the center of themselves and their relationship the couple can be helped to make their relationship explicit. All of us enter relationships with implicit and hidden contracts as well—will there be children? Who is to raise them? Will we remain close to our parents? Ministers can help bring these hidden contracts to the surface where they can be confirmed, denied, or reconstructed. In the wedding process the couple not only publish their own unique covenant for the world but also become aware of their real covenant themselves.

Finally, the appropriate intervention of the church occurs in blessing both partners as they seek to be open to God's creative powers in their union. With this emphasis we return to the church's original participation in wedding ceremonies. In light of the couple's own profession at this time, however, it is helpful to add a special commitment by the church community—that it be open to the gifts the couple will bring to the church out of the mystery of their journey. The church takes its stand as a recipient of their gifts rather than as a regulator of their path. The church community assembles to bless the bond.

Profession: Public Vocation

Marital communion has an intrinsic tie with public communication. Its private processes of communication also flow forth in forms of public vocation. Highlighting this affinity in the face of privatistic interpretations of marital union has been a major purpose of this book. Moreover, couples need to pursue their vocation not only as individuals but also as couples. This joint vocation should not be restricted to their calling as parents but should be expanded to other areas of public life.

Churches can assist this vocational thrust in three ways. First, they can give more ritual attention to people's entry into a discipline for public life, whether that be in an occupation, public office, or volunteer activity. This commitment is a sacramental act. It is a way that God gracefully reshapes a corrupted but hopeful creation. In their ceremonial observance of this fact churches can "commission" people into these various areas of life, just as missionaries are often commissioned. The concept of commissioning might be a better term for this action than "ministry," since ministry connotes intrachurch service, while commissioning is an act of sending out.

Second, this commissioning does not stop with a sacramental rite. It continues with churches providing opportunities for people pursuing related vocations to support each other, discern faith challenges, and respond to ethical demands. More of the educational life of the church should be given over to the issues arising from the vocational life of those it has commissioned.

Third, churches together with other associations should work more concertedly to make occupational life amenable to the demands of vocation—whether for individuals or for couples. We must move beyond the exploitation of the corporate wife (not to mention the pastoral wife) even as we move beyond the exploitation of the secretary. We need to open up more ways that occupational life can enhance marital partnership rather than tear it apart. Here indeed we are groping for strategies with a vision only misty in our eyes, but it is a direction we must take to honor the theological significance of marital communion and vocation.

Profession: Parental Vocation

Parenthood is both a covenantal act and a vocation deeply bound to the redemptive purposes of the church. In light of the construction I have advanced here we can see three ways churches can support parental action.

First, with the birth of a baby the parents enter into a special kind of covenant not only with the child but with the community of faith and the society at large. Churches can give this sacramental act ceremonial visibility. They can draw up a parental covenant shared by the whole community into which parents enter in bringing their baby into the life of the church. This could combine elements of infant baptism and dedication of babies, as found in many Baptist churches. Here the parents and the community covenant together to raise the child in openness to God's grace and the world around them.[15]

The second step, which is already well-attested among the churches, is the ongoing nurture, education, and formation of the child, keeping in mind his or her particular needs. Exploration of the field of Christian education is beyond our purview here.[16] One point, however, bears mention. Marriage as communion demands adequate individuation and the development of appropriate skills, not merely of household management, but of intimacy and communication. Churches would do well to offer increased opportunities to young people to engage in service activities in their early twenties. Apart from the mission impact of these efforts, they provide a time of moratorium and formation of identity before entering into serious sexual partnerships. The benefits in marital maturity and subsequent parental stability could be enormous.

Finally, churches can assist both parents in carrying on their parental covenant if their marriage dissolves. Some aspects of this are widely known—providing child-care centers that are more than warehouses, clearing away discrimination against single mothers, and assisting the women, men, and children struggling in violent relationships.

Other needs may not be as visible. Christians need to struggle against the stigmas that keep men from being adequate parents— whether these be cultural images or occupational straitjackets. Fathers and mothers should be enabled to share parental responsibilities in divorce as well as in marriage. Laws concerning custody need to honor and enhance the parental covenant, rather than exclude one parent. We should be clear about the difference between a single-parent family and a single-parent household. Churches can help forge new language and symbols to enhance the parental bond and help us grasp the variety of parental patterns.

All of these practical directives constitute as much an invitation as a demand. They are prospects to explore, practices to develop. It is in the thicket of these particulars that we can begin to map the new terrain we have entered in this exploration.

NOTES

1. The history of the concept of nature is a very tortured one. An introductory analysis appropriate to my concerns is Arthur Lovejoy, *Reflections on Human Nature* (Baltimore: Johns Hopkins Press, 1961). For the concept of action, see Richard Bernstein, *Praxis and Action: Contemporary Philosophies of Human Activity* (Philadelphia: University of Pennsylvania Press, 1971), and Nikolaus Lobkowicz, *Theory and Practice: History of a Concept from Aristotle to Marx* (Notre Dame, Ind.: University of Notre Dame Press, 1967).

My own construction is heavily influenced by Hannah Arendt, *The Human Condition* (Garden City, N.Y.: Doubleday Anchor Books, 1958) and *On Revolution* (New York: Viking Press, 1965); George Herbert Mead, *Mind, Self, and Society*, ed. Charles W. Morris (Chicago: University of Chicago Press, 1934); and Jürgen Habermas, *Theory and Practice* (Boston: Beacon Press, 1973). For a guide to Habermas, see Thomas McCarthy, *The Critical Theory of Jürgen Habermas* (Cambridge: M.I.T. Press, 1978).

2. John Haughey presents a sensitive discussion of this problem in *Should Anyone Say Forever? On Making, Keeping and Breaking Commitments* (New York: Doubleday & Co., 1975). See also Jack Dominion, *Marriage, Faith and Love* (New York: Crossroad, 1982), 97–99.

3. Perhaps the best known premarital inventory is the *Premarital Inventory* (1975) by Bess Associates, Casper, Wyoming, developed by Charles K. Burnett, et al. For an excellent pastoral approach, see John L. C. Mitman, *Premarital Counseling: A Manual for Clergy and Counselors* (New York: Seabury Press, 1980).

For the enrichment programs of Marriage Encounter (National), see George Roleder, ed., *Marriage Means Encounter* (Dubuque, Iowa: William C. Brown, 1973), and Don Demarest and Marilyn and Jerry Sexton, *Marriage Encounter: A Guide to Sharing* (New York: Carillon Books, 1977).

The connection between interpersonal and more public communication emerges in the work of Gerard Egan and Michael Cowan. See *People in Systems: A Model for Development in the Human-Service Professions and Education* (Monterey, Calif.: Brooks/Cole, 1979).

Dieter Hessel presents a full-blown, practical approach to social ministry that takes account of its psychological and spiritual ramifications in *Social Ministry* (Philadelphia: Westminster Press, 1982). This is an area that needs further attention with regard to marriage.

4. Please pardon the metaphorical use of Genesis here! While the psychological reduction from biblical "house" and tribal "flesh" to intimate resonance is not appropriate, the concern for the difference between a Freudian focus on parent-child relations and a Piagetian one on siblings is. For the Freudian focus, see *The Ego and the Id*, trans. Joan Riviere (New York: W. W. Norton, 1962), chap. 3; and in its recent form, Christopher Lasch, *Haven in a Heartless World: The Family Besieged* (New York: Basic Books, 1977), where parental authority is central. Piaget's views are in *The Moral Judgment of the Child*, trans. Marjorie Gabain (New York: Free Press, 1965).

5. The ancient Hebrews had no concept or practice of adoption, though it was practiced by other Semitic groups. They did not reflect on the fact that sonship by election, rather than physical generation, implied an adoptive relationship. St. Paul introduces adoption as a central theological concept in his letters to the Romans, Ephesians, and Galatians. In its Roman roots, see Fustel de Coulanges (chap. 1 n. 3), and Henry Maine, *Ancient Law* (Boston: Beacon Press, 1963), 125.

6. A secularized plea for this Puritan model emerges from W. Norton Grubb and Marvin Lazerson, *Broken Promises: How Americans Fail Their Children* (New York: Basic Books, 1982). The authors argue for a

theory of "public love" for children and a collective parental responsibility for the welfare of children.

For an excellent treatment of the ethics of parenthood from a philosophical perspective, see Jeffrey Blustein, *Parents and Children: The Ethics of the Family* (New York and London: Oxford University Press, 1982).

7. The triangle theory of family dynamics is well entrenched in systems theory. The failure of a dyadic interchange, as between husband and wife, draws in a third party—a child—to resolve or stabilize the situation. For Murray Bowen's systems theory, see Vincent Foley, "Family Therapy," in *Current Psychotherapies*, ed. Raymond Corsini (2d ed.; Itasca, Ill.: F. E. Peacock, 1979), 460–99. Bowen's approach is well utilized in *The Family Life Cycle: A Framework for Family Therapy*, ed. Elizabeth Carter and Monica McGoldrick (New York: Halsted Press, 1980). For the theory of system boundaries and individual differentiation, see Salvador Minuchin, *Families and Family Therapy* (Cambridge: Harvard University Press, 1974). William M. Walsh presents a comparative survey of family therapies in *A Primer in Family Therapy* (Springfield, Ill.: Charles C. Thomas, 1980).

The systems approach is placed within a theology of creation and call by Herbert Anderson in *A Theology for the Family* (Philadelphia: Fortress Press, 1984).

8. The argument for joint custody asserts that the destruction of the marital bond should not also destroy the parental bond. At present the disposition of the parental bond is thrown to the state, which then "awards" it to one or in some situations to both of the parents. The movement to disturb these bonds as little as possible by requiring joint custodial arrangements is now widespread. The best survey is Ciji Ware, *Sharing Parenthood After Divorce: An Enlightened Custody Guide for Mothers, Fathers, and Kids* (New York: Viking Press, 1982). For a fuller ethical presentation, see my "Shared Parenthood in Divorce: The Parental Covenant and Custody Law," *Journal of Law and Religion* 2.1 (1984). A collection of key articles and an overview of the legal situation is provided in *Joint Custody and Shared Parenting*, ed. Jay Folberg (Portland, Oreg.: The Association of Family and Conciliation Courts; and Washington, D.C.: Bureau of National Affairs, Inc., 1984).

9. Parker Palmer explores the connection between mystical communion, especially as it appears in Quaker traditions, and public action in his stimulating book, *The Company of Strangers* (New York: Crossroad, 1981). Palmer touches on the household and family, however, rather than the impact of marital communion.

10. Max Stackhouse highlights the innovative thrust of vocation in *Ethics and the Urban Ethos* (Boston: Beacon Press, 1972), 142–49, 184–89. The emphasis on order can be found in Emil Brunner, *The Divine Imperative*, trans. Olive Wyon (Philadelphia: Westminster Press, 1947), book II, xx.

11. Grubb and Lazerson, *Broken Promises,* and Degler, *At Odds* (see chap. 1 n. 5) as well as Ann Oakley, *Subject Women* (New York: Pantheon Books, 1981).

The bias against spouses sharing jobs or working in the same organization arose in order to serve organizational "rationality." The barriers against this vocational expression are lessening but are still quite strong. Jane Hood provides helpful concepts and case studies of changing patterns of work and family in *Becoming a Two-Job Family* (New York: Frederick A. Praeger, 1983).

12. This view of sacrament is heavily influenced by the work of anthropologists such as Mary Douglas, *Natural Symbols: Explorations in Cosmology* (New York: Pantheon Books, 1970), and Raymond Firth, *Symbols: Public and Private* (Ithaca, N.Y.: Cornell University Press, 1973); and sociologists like Hugh D. Duncan, *Communication and Social Order* (New York and London: Oxford University Press, 1968). See also James D. Shaughnessy, ed., *Roots of Ritual* (Grand Rapids: Wm. B. Eerdmans, 1973), especially the articles by Brian Wicker and Christopher Crocker.

13. For a comparative and analytical approach to these therapies, see W. Everett and T. J. Bachmeyer, *Disciplines in Transformation: A Guide to Theology and the Behavioral Sciences* (Washington, D.C.: University Press of America, 1979). Don Browning provides theological and ethical analyses of some key issues in *Religious Thought and the New Psychologies* (Philadelphia: Fortress Press, 1985).

14. The interchange between pastoral counseling and church administration needs more attention. For sensitivity to this dimension, see Arthur Adams, *Effective Leadership for Today's Church* (Philadelphia: Westminster Press, 1978), Richard G. Hutcheson, Jr., *Wheel Within the Wheel: Confronting the Management Crisis of the Pluralistic Church* (Atlanta: John Knox Press, 1979), Lyle E. Schaller and Charles Tidwell, *Creative Church Administration* (Nashville: Abingdon Press, 1975), and Jerry Woffard and Kenneth Kilinski, *Organization and Leadership in the Local Church* (Grand Rapids: Zondervan, 1973).

15. For openings to this kind of practice in the Roman Catholic Church, see *The Rite of Christian Initiation of Adults* (Washington, D.C.: U.S. Catholic Conference, 1974), and Aidan Kavanaugh, *The Shape of Baptism: The Rite of Christian Initiation* (New York: Pueblo Publishing, 1978). The Baptist ritual of dedicating children is drawn from the Gospel account in Luke 2:21–39. The only full treatment of this practice that I know of is "A Baptist Interpretation of the Rite of Dedication: A Resource for Ministry," by James A. Braker (D. Min. thesis, Colgate Rochester Divinity School, 1982).

16. For a direction congenial to the one advanced here, see Thomas H. Groome, *Christian Religious Education* (New York: Harper & Row, 1980).